DAVID THOMSON *on*

THE
A L I E N
QUARTET

Bloomsbury Movie Guides

DAVID THOMSON *on*

THE
ALIEN
QUARTET

Bloomsbury Movie Guide No.4

BLOOMSBURY

ACKNOWLEDGMENTS

I am grateful to Matthew Hamilton for asking me to write this book; to David Reynolds and Michael Jones, also at Bloomsbury; to Jorge Saralegui and Vincent Ward, for talking about the films; to Nick Scudamore, for a fascinating, unpublished articles on the subject; to Mary Corliss for help with stills; to Lorraine Latorraca, Tony Safford and to my family. And to Laura Morris for having it all work out.

First published in 1998

Bloomsbury Publishing Plc, 38 Soho Square, London W1V 5DF

A CIP catalogue record for this book is available from the British Library

ISBN 0 7475 3803 4

10 9 8 7 6 5 4 3 2 1

Typeset by Palimpsest Book Production Limited,
Polmont, Stirlingshire

Printed in England by Clays Ltd, St Ives plc

For NICHOLAS and ZACHARY

not so much aliens as allies

CONTENTS

Sometimes the arrangement of mortal hostility is
hard to distinguish from that of an embrace.

Once Upon a Time . . .

Where do films come from? Where do they go? After a hundred years of movie, we are still not very adept at answering those questions. Let alone the matter of what they do to us while they are 'here'. We have set explanations, and we agree more or less that certain arguments apply — that the business system of motion pictures delivers (or seeks to sell) these things to us; or that they may be the work of individuals, artists, *auteurs*, film-makers. Then, as for what they do, why they 'entertain' us — or not. They make us laugh, cry, hide our eyes, or cultivate our souls. They move us. As if we were so important. Or is it just time that is moving? Look back a hundred years or so in your own family history, say, beyond the lives of people you knew or heard of, beyond mere names, to the notional claim that the family tree had branches then. Were those people moved by stories or plays they encountered? Does it matter? I mean 'matter' besides the extraordinary, anonymous but undeniable thrust of life itself. What is left of their being moved? Is that load there in our spit, our blood or our come?

There is another explanation for movies — that they are a climate of story, or wonder, or mystery, eternally recurring, and that we go to the story to witness it. According to that notion, the story does not have to be 'good' or a 'masterwork'. It is just some act of telling that holds us and leaves us wondering. For it is not so much that we know what stories mean, as that we know we should ask that question. We would not ask if any answer was clear. And so we exist in a fruitful quandary, being ourselves, and watching shows called *Alien* and *Aliens* and asking, Are they messages? Or warnings?

This book tries to think about some of those questions by posing the idea of a unity. I am saying that *Alien* (1979), *Aliens* (1986), *Alien*[3] (1992) and *Alien Resurrection* (1997) are the four parts of a quartet, the four movements of a symphony, or just four chapters in one story. What assists that argument is the fact that all four were made by one company, 20th Century-Fox, and that they fix on one character, Ripley, always played by the actress Sigourney Weaver. But the films are not called *Ripley*, even if the story, from one film to another, fits and carries her forward. What counters the argument is the fact that the films were directed by different people, and that each one was made as a separate entity. Films 2, 3 and 4 were not thought of as 1, 2 and 3 were being made. No one planned a quartet. Even now, there is uncertainty as to whether there might be a 5. Yet a 5, surely, would alter any feeling of unity or shape in the quartet.

Nor am I suggesting that all four are good, let alone great, or satisfactory films. I might as well say now that after lengthy investigation and re-viewing, I suspect that *Alien* – as art, or something susceptible to critical account – is the best of the four. Further, I suspect that the line deteriorates or weakens steadily, thus illustrating the conventional Hollywood wisdom that sequels get worse and worse. *Alien Resurrection* is, by common consent, the poorest of the films; yet it may contain the most interesting development of the idea that lurks in all four. Of course, *Alien* has an extra claim for quality: it conjured up Ripley, the aliens and their struggle for the first time. It suggested that she and the beasts were there for each other. Every film that followed voiced a need to stay faithful to the 'classic' conception, and not just to keep faith with the audience. There was also some sense of a profound yet simple story structure having been discovered, or freed, that had to be honoured.

Even so, I am not sure that – and I am not saying that – *Alien* is a great film. It is 'only' something I have never been able to get out of my head – just as there are some things that, once admitted, can never be removed from the body. Story is such a thing, and that is how some stories get passed down and remain alive long after a family line has lost knowledge of those ancestors who may have started the story. So this is a book about story and its possibilities, one of which may be that any 'alien' thing must lose its apartness, and become more like us, the longer we look at it. Or is it that we absorb the alien?

Dan O'Bannon had the first idea – yet he likely had it because of a disagreement over where ideas came from, and who owned them. In August 1970, when he was twenty-four, O'Bannon got to talking with John Carpenter. They were fellow students in the graduate programme in film studies at the University of Southern California. Carpenter wanted O'Bannon to act in a student film he was making 'about four seedy astronauts in a small spaceship'. Five years later that project was released as *Dark Star*, a 50-minute student film that had been bumped up to 83 minutes (and from 16mm to 35mm) when the entrepreneur Jack H. Harris agreed to release it. O'Bannon did act in the film, but he had also done the screenplay with Carpenter, he had edited the picture, he had done much of the set design, and he had helped with the special effects.

Student films cannot help but be collaborative – and they often own up to it; big pictures are sometimes made in the same way, but they take distinct credits very seriously. O'Bannon asked Carpenter for a credit on *Dark Star* that would read, 'A film by John Carpenter and Dan O'Bannon'. But Carpenter insisted that he was the lone director, and he told O'Bannon that he never wanted to work with him again. Friends became rivals – aliens, even.

Dark Star is full of promise, humour and a love of its own budgetary austerity. It includes a scene in which the astronaut played by O'Bannon – his name is Pinback – smuggles an alien creature on board the ship to serve as mascot, or pet. But the alien escapes and proves so pesky that Pinback has to kill it.

It is very likely that by the time *Dark Star* was done, Carpenter and O'Bannon could not remember the turmoil of collaboration clearly enough to know who had thought of what. And it is probably true that O'Bannon – a fan and connoisseur of science fiction in all its forms – could not be sure what he had invented or absorbed from that idea-heavy genre. After all, he might have seen the 1958 movie *It! The Terror from Beyond Space*, written by Jerome Bixby and directed by Edward L. Cahn, in which a mission to Mars returns to Earth with one survivor. It is reasoned that he has killed all the others, but the true threat is a Martian secretly on board the ship.

Going a little further afield, in the mid-1950s in Britain there was a television series, later made into a movie, written by Nigel Kneale, *The Quatermass Experiment*, in which a sole survivor from space travel begins to turn into slime and fungus, and so has to be destroyed. One could go further, evidently: in science fiction, the worlds out there are sometimes a field of daydreams; but far more often they become projections of nightmare, paranoia and our worst imaginings. The least likely thing to happen in science fiction is the condition most apparent in the real space travel we have observed so far – nothing. And even nothing, in story, can weigh upon the melancholy soul until it feels turned inside out.

One year before Carpenter and O'Bannon first talked about what became *Dark Star*, Neil Armstrong walked on the Moon. That was the dramatic climax (or anti-climax) in an approximately thirty-year history of space on TV, going from Gagarin and Glenn all the way to the *Challenger* disaster. All the movies have found to film from that real story was *The Right Stuff* (a fine film, but a failure) and *Apollo 13* (a very routine film, but a hit because of its convincing recreation of the real peril). Nothing else, and clearly that is because so little actually happened in space.

Yet, as the American space programme built, the real technology (and the rather drained, grey quality of the astronauts and their language) was a tremendous inspiration for, or pressure on, movies. One does not have to think that *2001: A Space Odyssey* (1968) walks on water – indeed, maybe it is paralysed in aspic – but no one can question its influence. For one thing, sci-fi was made respectable by the grand designs and portentous attention of Stanley Kubrick. And, whatever else, his movie uncovered an edge of mystery and loneliness in space – things that are very important to the *Alien* movies where there is no unshakeable faith in human culture keeping its place (and apparent primacy) in the infinite darkness.

There's room for debate as to whether *2001* thinks optimistically of human history or not, though its human creatures are the numbest and blankest in even Kubrick's work. In the same year, 20th Century-Fox launched a franchise, set in the future, yet largely free from special effects: *Planet of the Apes* (1968), *Beneath the Planet of the Apes* (1970) and *Escape from the Planet of the Apes* (1971) were effective box-office performers that neatly reversed the supposed natural order of things. The remake of *King Kong* (1976) – laughed at by most critics, but a smash hit – had a far more sentimental view of simian emotions.

But then, in 1977, two films altered the place of science fiction, just as they introduced a new generation to power in the movies, as well as a new scale of business. George Lucas's *Star Wars* opened in May 1977: budgeted at $10 million, it had gone $1 million over in costs, and it did not much impress the Fox power structure. It earned $3.5 million in nine days; $165 million in its first run; and rentals – i.e., revenue back to Fox – of $250 million by the end of 1980. Beyond the movie's direct income, there was another fortune made in the merchandising of toys and souvenirs – an area that Lucas had kept for himself in the contract.

To put things in perspective: *Star Wars* in its first release period took in twice as much money as *The Godfather* had done only five years earlier. It took in $35 million more than *Jaws* had earned in 1975. And *Star Wars* was radiantly optimistic, a delirious mixture of movie technology and comic-book attitudes and story-lines. Another vein of optimism was shown at the end of 1977 when Columbia released Steven Spielberg's *Close Encounters of the Third Kind*, a movie that draws upon every bizarre report of aliens looking at Earth, and found them as wise and friendly as . . . well, as *E.T.*, a few years later. *Close Encounters* earned rentals of $77 million in its first run. (Five years later, *E.T.* itself had rentals of $187 million.) The business has never been the same since, and in hindsight it's clear that *Jaws* and *Star Wars* and *Close Encounters* were the clarion announcements of a new age. By 1979, strenuous imitation or duplication was the order of the day: *Superman* earned $81 million; *Star Trek – The Motion Picture*, the first movie from a TV series that had prospered from 1966 to 1969, made $35 million. And *Alien* earned $40 million.

That certainly explains why *Alien* came to be made – but it draws attention to what separates it from the films of Lucas and Spielberg. Dan O'Bannon's script (called *Starbeast*) was taken up by a 'producer', Ronald Shusett, who himself contributed to the script. (Shusett had no credits as a producer, but he had a story credit on the 1973 picture *W.*) A development deal was made with Fox, and Gordon Carroll, a more experienced producer, came on board. Carroll, who was fifty, had worked on *The World of Suzie Wong* (1960), *Cool Hand Luke* (1967) and *Pat Garrett and Billy the Kid* (1973). Indeed, the latter film had been Carroll's idea: he had commissioned the script and then enticed Sam Peckinpah to direct it. Carroll had a company, Brandywine, in which Walter Hill and David Giler were partners. It was Walter Hill who took up *Starbeast*, saw some potential – as well as amateurish writing – and did the polish that got Fox involved.

At that stage, Fox were cautious about the picture. They thought it might be a $1 million movie, and at that level O'Bannon was likely hopeful that he could direct it as a kind of sequel to *Dark Star* – small, funky, with spacemen as grunts, comic but alarming. Carroll saw more potential in the very simple story, the claustrophobia and a monster that could be more than just alarming. The notion was there already that *Alien* might not be science fiction; it was maybe a horror picture.

The two genres often overlap. After all, the fearsome imagination of Dr Frankenstein (a great, wayward, scientist) made the horror of the monster. (And then that story found pathos in the creature that had never asked for life.) Time and again, in sci-fi, genius has produced monsters of reason. But the horror genre knows we do not need science to dream of terrible dark shapes and forces. Our deepest nature summons them, and with it the delicious dread – call it religious or psychological – that we deserve them, and cannot function without them. Thus, in *Alien*, a bored, jaded crew finds their monster and suddenly their destiny is manifest. Most are lost, but one becomes a legendary heroine.

Once in development, Carroll and Fox sought more serious rewrites from David Giler (who had credits on a wide range of films from *Myra Breckenridge* to *The Parallax View* to *Fun with Dick and Jane*) and Walter Hill.

Hill was a director already: he had made *Hard Times* (1975) and *The Driver* (1978). As well as writing those projects, he had had writing credits on Peckinpah's *The Getaway* (1972), *The Thief Who Came to Dinner* (1973), *The Mackintosh Man* (1973), and *The Drowning Pool* (1975). Hill was famous for writing in the present tense, without wasting time on motivation or background: he wrote action in such a way that you 'got' the character. 'I don't care where people come from,' he said. 'I don't care where they are going. I do care *what* they are doing. I care very much. I think that excluding what happened before our drama starts and also what will happen after our drama ends makes the screen characterisation much more refined.'

Gordon Carroll called this process a mix of 'blank verse and staccato', and it was clearly the transformation that turned *Alien* into not just a makeable film, but a more expensive one. Together, Giler and Hill amended the crew from all-male to five men and two women. They also invented their names. And rather than stress the ship's computer, 'Mother' – a very Kubrickian device – they introduced a robot, Ash, who kept many of the computer's lines. Carroll hoped to persuade Hill to direct the picture, but Hill felt he knew too little about space or science fiction. He wanted to go off and do a Western. Several other directors turned the project down.

It was then that Sandy Lieberson, in charge of European production for Fox, suggested Ridley Scott as a possible director. Scott was English and forty years old in 1977. Born in South Shields, he was educated at the West Hartlepool College of Art and then the Royal College of Art. A set designer for BBC-TV, he had turned to directing (he worked on *Z Cars* and *The Informer*) and did many successful commercials in a company formed with his brother, Tony, before making his first feature film, *The Duellists* in 1977. A story of the Napoleonic era, it featured a prolonged rivalry between two officers, played by Harvey Keitel and Keith Carradine. Though the picture did modestly commercially, it attracted attention because of its spectacular visual quality and because of the aura of fatalism drawn from the original Conrad novella.

Scott was hoping to do a movie of *Tristan and Isolde* – he has never done it yet. But as he prepared it, he saw *Star Wars* and was captivated. It convinced him to be interested in science fiction, a genre that hitherto had left him unmoved. He read the *Alien* script in forty minutes – 'It was just Bang! Woompf! Straight through. It was unpretentious, very violent, yet a lot of character painting came through, and I just felt it was an amazing piece of entertainment. Also, to me, it was more than a horror film, it is a film about *terror*.' Scott signed on to make the picture. Its budget mounted. And sooner or later, at his behest, the decision was made to do the bulk of the shooting in Britain.

Before then, in America, Ridley Scott spent time with O'Bannon and Ronald Shusett (who continued to function as a team). They had ideas about the look of the film, and it was they who first showed Scott samples of the work of the artist, H. R. Giger★, notably the book *Necronomicron*. Indeed, Scott saw one picture in that book and felt he had found the ideal for his *Alien* (it had blank eyes, fierce teeth, hands, a vast back end to its head and a phallic tail). O'Bannon came back as an important voice at this point – far more than Walter Hill, say. He knew science fiction, the work of Giger, and had experimented with its look. O'Bannon would end up with another credit on the movie – 'Visual Design Consultant' – and he got his friend Ron Cobb on the picture. Cobb had worked on *Dark Star*, and he would be a 'concept artist' on *Alien*. Scott liked their notion, derived from *Dark Star*, that the *Nostromo* was a rather shabby, old ship, not a Kubrickian grand hotel:

> The look really was meant to reflect the crew members, who, I felt, should be like truck drivers in space. Their jobs, which took them on several-year journeys through space, were to them a normal state of affairs . . . We project a not-too-distant future in which there are many vehicles tramping around the universe, on mining expeditions, erecting military installations, or whatever . . . These ships . . . look used, beat-up, covered with graffiti, and uncomfortable.

★Hans Giger was Swiss, born in Chur in 1940, an industrial designer and a painter whose surreal visions had already attracted film-makers. Thus, he did designs for the 1969 *Swiss Made*, and collaborated with Alexandro Jodorowsky on the attempt to film Frank Herbert's *Dune* – subsequently made by David Lynch.

Scott saw the crew of the *Nostromo* as similarly fatigue-ridden. Even if a computer had once selected this crew on grounds of compatibility, they had become exhausted by prolonged company. As he prepared, Scott was especially interested in the way people might be affected by claustrophobia, melancholy and the inescapable company of unwanted fellows. He liked the way the script had them talking and arguing because it suggested the underlying tension. He also removed a scene where Dallas and Ripley at least discussed having sex – as a relief. Scott felt that the scene was unbelievable, coming after the first full display of the monster's powers. But he also believed in a crew of people who had become too isolated, or alienated, from conventional contact. Still, that left space, or energy, for some underground sense of attraction between Ripley and the alien: truly, a seed of the series. In interviews, Scott has always seemed surprised at suggestions of a sexual undercurrent between Ripley and the alien – but he did not need to see it; he had created the dead emotional climate on the *Nostromo* that let such a feeling flower. Not everything in art is designed, or intended.

Indeed, in O'Bannon's first script the crew members had been written in such a way that they might be men or women. Sexuality or gender were no longer distinguishing marks. It was in the Hill–Giler rewrites that Ripley and Lambert were identified as females, though they still had very little sexual 'colouring'. However, that choice ensured that a woman would be the last and lone survivor, and surely Scott had a decisive influence on that. For it is clear now that Ridley Scott has an uncommon interest in strong women who shape their own lives, stand up for themselves, and lay equal claim to the soldier's life. The great love story of *Tristan and Isolde* may have evaded Scott, but he has given us the two women in *Someone to Watch Over Me*, *Thelma & Louise*, Caroline Goodall's wife in the neglected *White Squall*, and *G.I. Jane* (a character who could easily have a picture of Ripley in her locker).

Only then did Sigourney Weaver come into play. She had little to offer at that time beyond herself, and the several plays she had appeared in. She gathered that Fox were resisting the idea of having a newcomer in the role, but she believed she had been recommended highly to Scott, to Carroll, to Giler and Hill – those were the men she met when she went in for interviews (for it was apparent that Giler and Hill had managed to be promoted up to the level of producers). Weaver had enough self-confidence not to be meek. She took it for granted that, if chosen, she would have a voice in refining her character, and she observed at the outset that it was a very bleak story where people didn't relate.

She met the ultimate powers at Fox at that time, Gareth Wigan and Alan Ladd, Jr., and they agreed she should make a test. For that, she flew to London where Scott had already rigged up a version of the *Nostromo* as a set. They did a run-through of the whole script. 'I wore old Army surplus stuff . . . We didn't want it to look like *Jackie Onassis in Space*: we wanted to look more like pirates.'

Alan Ladd, Jr. looked at the tests and asked all the women he could find in the Fox office what they thought. They liked Weaver. The day after she got back to New York, she was told she had the part – for $33,000. The seven actors on the picture were hired for well under $500,000. But the casting was acute: with two English voices there was a vague sense of the crew being beyond nationality. Moreover, in Yaphet Kotto, Harry Dean Stanton, Ian Holm, John Hurt and Tom Skerritt they had some of the best supporting actors around. Kotto had lately starred in *Blue Collar*; Holm had enormous experience on stage and screen; Stanton had been seen recently in *The Missouri Breaks*, *Straight Time* and *Wise Blood*; Hurt had made *The Shout* and *Midnight Express*; and Skerritt was known from *M.A.S.H.* and *The Turning Point*.

As Weaver told journalist Danny Peary several years later, she had a simple sense of Ripley:

She's a very matter-of-fact person. I think she grew up believing there is a certain order to things that could not be broken or changed. She had very rational training. And her beliefs are exploded in the film when she suddenly has to work on instinct and emotion rather then intellect . . . Actually, the part I wanted to play was Lambert, Veronica Cartwright's part. In the first script I read, she just cracked jokes the whole time. What was wonderful about it was that here was a woman who was wise-assing, telling stupid jokes just when everyone else was getting hysterical . . . The character changed, however, when Ridley and Veronica decided to give viewers a sympathetic character.

In other interviews, in the years since, Weaver has suggested that she reckons Ripley was married on Earth and even that she had a daughter – things never referred to, but valuable in helping an actress find a role and indicators of her latent emotional needs.

So there was a cast without a star, a set of brilliant or very promising actors hired to play rather drab people. There was the *Nostromo*, that cross between a truck and a tramp steamer in space. But there was a star in the script and the concept – a villain whose entry was delayed, like that of Harry Lime in *The Third Man*, but who, once there, commanded the story and its mood. The alien. Didn't the title tell you it was his picture? Didn't his incarnation carry all the burden of shifting this venture from science fiction to horror?

H. R. Giger, the Swiss surrealist painter, had two tasks really. He had to design the landscape that the *Nostromo* crew found on the planet they are sent to investigate. It was the notion of the film that they found the wreck of a crashed spacecraft – they called it the *Derelict* – on the planet (yet no one ever worked out whether the crash had been an accident, or by design). But the *Derelict* was to be so large and strange that one might wonder whether it wasn't the entire landscape. Giger's drawings were so impressive that Fox added $2.5 million to the budget – to accommodate them, and to show confidence.

Giger proceeded according to instructions:

They asked me to design something which could not have been made by human beings – which is quite difficult! I tried to build it up with organic-looking parts – tubes, pipes, bones: a kind of Art Nouveau. Everything I designed in the film used the idea of bones. I made the model of the alien landscape with real bones and put it together with Plasticene, pipes and little pieces of motors. I mixed up technical and organic things. I call this 'biomechanics'.

Giger was obsessive, very sexual in most of his work, and an eager student of nightmare. More intriguingly, he believed in a world in which man's pre eminence was passing: 'Led astray by humanism and blinded by the belief that man is the centre of the universe, he fails to recognise his true place in the order of things. He forgets the basis of his existence, and therefore he must perish.'

That set was built at the Bray Studio, several miles away from Shepperton, where the *Nostromo* scenes were filmed. As for the alien, it was derived from the forms Giger had imagined for the *Derelict*. But the alien was always conceived as a dynamic creature, one that grew very rapidly, changing shape and size. Giger made the full-grown monster itself, with the aid of Carlo Rambaldi (who had created the 1976 King Kong, and who would make E.T. in a few years' time). It was Ridley Scott's contribution to the cult of the monster – to its terror, and the sense of its inevitable victory – that he never quite let us see it whole, or from a distance. We saw details in sudden, alarming close-ups that left so much more to the imagination.

The movies depend on showing us things, but the tradition of horror (or shock) films learned early on that there was a special power and threat in withholding the horrific thing. The producer Val Lewton made a series of remarkable films in the 1940s (*Cat People*, *I Walked With a Zombie*) that turned on hideous things arising in ordinary life.

Partly for reasons of economy, but also out of mischief and insight, Lewton saw the value in keeping the fearsome thing unseen – so that imagination would work. Show a shock and it begins to be viewable, acceptable, familiar . . . stale. That logic has seldom failed. But in a series of films the horrible sight risks becoming known (un-alien) or increasingly vile and loathsome. That balance is central to the *Alien* films.

The small monsters, the hand that grips Kane's face and then the fish-like creature that bursts from his chest, were the responsibility of Roger Dicken, though Giger liked to suggest that he had supervised Dicken's work and helped him in difficult areas. There was emerging by this time in the film industry a serious rivalry between effects artists as to who could create the most appalling and most articulated monsters. Giger was eager to make a larger career for himself in movie-making, and he was a very dramatic artist, dressed all in black leather as he presided over his own astonishing set.

In allowing the picture to be shot in England, Fox made it easier for Scott to hire several people who had played important roles on *Star Wars*. John Mollo was enlisted to design the space suits and some other costumes. Roger Christian and Les Dilley were recruited as art designers.

And so *Alien* was shot, by Derek Vanlint and Denys Ayling, over a period of four months, starting on July 25th, 1978, for $9 million. Scott himself frequently operated the camera, and that left Weaver feeling that he risked neglecting the actors. David Giler and Gordon Carroll were in attendance most of the time. Hill was there for post-production. O'Bannon was there at first, but he got into trouble making computer print-outs and he was sent away. The picture itself, edited by Terry Rawlings and Peter Weatherly, and with music by Jerry Goldsmith★ and from Howard Hanson's 2nd

---

★Goldsmith had previously written the music for *Freud*, *A Patch of Blue*, *The Sand Pebbles*, *Planet of the Apes*, *Patton*, *Papillon*, *Chinatown* and *The Omen*.

Symphony,* opened on May 25th, 1979, two years to the day after the opening of *Star Wars*.

Who can judge the effects of contemporaneity? Still, *Alien* is a film about time and eternity, so it may not be irrelevant to say that it was made and refined as President Carter, Anwar Sadat and Menachem Begin made an agreement at Camp David; as an earthquake in Iran killed 25,000; as Cardinal Wojtyla became Pope John Paul II; as 911 deaths occurred when the members of the People's Temple killed themselves in Jonestown, Guyana; as a nuclear accident occurred at Three Mile Island in Pennsylvania – why is it that we remember disasters? Only today it is reported that a huge explosion has been detected in space – maybe 12 billion light years away. No one knows what it was. But if it had been closer – just a few thousand light years – we would be gone.

Who made *Alien*, then? I hope that this brief history has identified many authors: Dan O'Bannon and Ronald Shusett for thinking of it in the first place; Gordon Carroll for carrying it along; Walter Hill and David Giler for making a persuasive shooting script and for defining the eventual characters; H. R. Giger for a unique vision; Sigourney Weaver for the upright common-sense look she gave it; Carlo Rambaldi for making the cruel head work; Ridley Scott for presiding over all these things and choosing most of them. Alan Ladd, Jr. for saying OK. And so many others, from Yaphet Kotto to Howard Hanson, from Ron Cobb to Garth Thomas, who was production manager, to Bolaji Badejo, a 6 ft 10 in Nigerian art student, who wore the alien costume in many shots just because he happened to bump into an agent in a London pub.

*Howard Hanson (1896–1981) was a composer, teacher and conductor, born in Wahoo, Nebraska. His 2nd Symphony – the 'Romantic' – premiered in November 1930. The reconciliatory theme that emerges in the first movement was used in the last moments of the film with Ripley safe and homeward-bound.

Sometimes that many people make for muddle and disaster. Sometimes the crowd becomes something like a team. On *Alien* there was all the tension of any big production when cumbersome sets and effects are involved, along with large sums of money, and when, after a certain point, everyone just wants the damn thing to be over. Not everything ends harmoniously. The first instinct of the producers was to ignore O'Bannon's credit. He had to fight. But when the Writers Guild made their arbitration decision on the writing credits, they awarded them to O'Bannon and Shusett, largely because Giler and Hill were by then co-producers and the Guild is always averse to awarding that breed writing credit. O'Bannon and Shusett deserve a credit, but it is entirely unfair that Hill and Giler were omitted.

And, of course, the picture needed us. The film only worked when we saw it. It needed to be a show. Danny Peary once asked Ridley Scott whether, near the end of the picture, the alien sneaked into the shuttle because it knew the main ship was about to blow or because it was steadfastly following Ripley? That is a fascinating question, one that probes the nature and thrust of the alien intelligence. But the director had solved it by heeding a quite different imperative: indeed, his decision left the question hanging.

'Because we needed an end to the picture,' said Scott.

ALIEN

1

The pale blue upright of 'I' appears at the centre of the top of the screen – it might be the letter or a distant view of some immense space enterprise, even the tablet in *2001*. But slowly the word 'ALIEN' will stretch across the top of the screen, above the terse opening credits, as the image crawls from left to right over what could be a view of deep space, with diagonal skeins of light, or aura, in it; or limbs as seen close up, and slightly out of focus. Jerry Goldsmith's music has some distant tone; even further away there are muffled drums and a wistful woodwind theme. The pace of the music seems linked to that of the crawl – in other words, from the very outset there is a promise of control, something like fate that runs space; that or story-telling.

The names of the actors appear in this order – and surely order has to do with meaning – upper- and lower-case names, all solus: Tom Skerritt/Sigourney Weaver/Veronica Cartwright/Harry Dean Stanton/John Hurt/Ian Holm/Yaphet Kotto 'as Parker'. What intrigues about that order is the difficulty of identifying its meaning.

There is then a view of some form in space – it is a composition of mottled blue greys against a solid, darker blue. Is it the ship? Information conveyed in titles suggest that, but the shot is still mysterious, for the thing seems static, and its mottling, its variegation, its somewhat gnarled look, will find other claimants later. But the information is very blunt: 'The *Nostromo*, with a crew of seven, is headed home (or returning to) earth [not Earth] with 20,000,000 tons of mineral ore.' And then, far below, moving right to left (i.e., against the first movement), we see the ship (a model, if you like, a toy even), a vast, serried shape, with smoke-stacks, suggesting enormous capacity and sophistication and not unredolent of *Star Wars*. It is moving, quite rapidly, on its determined course. The deep tone grows stronger, but

there are faraway strings now, as if the ship did represent some mark
of intelligence, civilisation or yearning – or all three, why not? Why
travel through that dark, empty space without some desire or purpose?
Some sense of things waiting to be known?

We cut to an empty, yet ultra-modern interior, and the movement
of the craft as seen from below is picked up in a track or zooming out-
wards (it is not clear which) to show a corridor. The camera comes to
the elbow and then looks down another arm of similar corridor. There
are pipes, vents in the walls, as well as what seems like padded leather
cushioning. And the corridors have an approximately octagonal form
– they are in line with the spaceship interiors of *2001*.

We see a working table, and though the camera pans away there is
time to notice a jacket draped loosely over a chair, and also one of those
toy dipping birds – it *is* dipping – of the sort that is set in motion by
liquid. We scan more corridor and rows of blank control screens. Then
some instrument on a table bumps (there is clear movement) and papers
flap: this brief action is unexplained, though it does not feel sinister. And
then we see helmets – like empty heads – which are emergency helmets
lined up, waiting for use. Out of focus, behind them, there is some other
bobbing motion – sometimes I wonder if it is the cat, Jones, but could
the cat survive on the ship while the crew slept?

In the visor of a helmet, we see a computer screen come to life with
the signal message, 'Nostromo 180924609'. Other signals follow.

The image fades out – as if to say *this* is the *Nostromo*, sailing along,
serene yet somehow with an air of having been abandoned. Then it
fades back and we see strip lighting come on as the camera turns away
to show an octagonal door. The door slides up and flimsy white coats
hanging next to it flutter in its draft.

Inside this chamber there are six – we will realise there must be a
seventh – coffin-like bunks with glass or plastic lids. The lids rise in
unison and we see figures lying on their backs in the white padded
interiors. We notice white men, and one black. We do not see
women, or notice them.

But one figure, John Hurt, begins to wake. He wears either underpants or some kind of white loincloth. In a series of quick dissolves, we see him stand; we see him, eyes closed, absorb the air or renewed consciousness. The light on his body is very white. We seem to hear breathing. Other figures in the seven begin to stir.

2

Does the *Nostromo* need these crew members — or, if you call a ship *Nostromo*, are you somehow obliged to put people on it? And people large enough for destiny? I mean to say, isn't it within the claw-and-hammer technique of an efficient hulk like this (a commercial towing vehicle) to grab itself 20 million tons of ore, and have the electronic wit to get home? Do we need these human touches — like the jacket over the chair, a coffee cup on a console, those dipping beaks and these wan crew members awakening? Did the system have to go to all the fuss and expense of freezing them, too? How long are these voyages? And if they are so long that they test human lifespan or patience, isn't that one more reason to let the octagonal corridors make their sweet way through space without contamination? Or is it that there cannot be anything like story without the mess of people? What is message, but the culture left by untidy, anxious creatures? After all, without people, the ship would hardly need corridors.

These questions surely arise just because of the tranquillity of the opening, and the lovely spectacle of process and journeying, both of which have momentum, duration and their own ritual, even if, as yet, they lack that quaint hobby-horse, the arc, story.

3

Even as we see the sleeping crew awaken, we hear their desultory chatter at the meal table — which is where the final dissolve takes us. The camera slides in at table-top level, and circles to show the crew members held together in the white light of the table. We see rectangular containers of brightly coloured foods – or their artificial substitute. We see Jones, the ginger cat, on the table, feeding; and those two feathered birds, dipping their beaks down still, which Jones has learned to ignore.

We see a bored, formless group. One cannot tell its chain of command, or identify a commander. In fact, in the table's banter, Parker (Yaphet Kotto) and Brett (Harry Dean Stanton) are most prominent, and they are seen in looming close-ups, with other people behind them and smaller. They are a pair, a team; Brett wears a crew cap; they slap high fives together. When Kane (John Hurt) says he feels dead, Parker drawls back, 'Anyone tell you you look dead?' and the line gets a laugh. There are two women in the group: Lambert (Veronica Cartwright), who fusses at her hair and complains of feeling cold; and Ripley (Sigourney Weaver), still, watchful, amused and more focused. She seems to be the youngest member of the crew, and she enjoys Parker's joke about the way Kane looks. There's no indication of how long this crew has been a crew, but Ripley has enough of an eye and a smile to make one wonder whether she has a thing for Dallas (Tom Skerritt), the only possible guy on board – he is bearded, laid back, and with a sheen of weary experience.

But we don't know that he is the commander. He tells Parker to abide by the contract they all signed. But Parker and Brett are wryly agitating for a better share of the ore cargo. They are all assuming that they have been woken because they are nearly home now. Dallas refers to the contract without any real assertion of authority. There are no 'sirs', and so on, no orders, no structure. The talk is untidy, too; lines slip across each other, and it is not easy to discern what has been said.

But there is a gentle claxon sound, and instantly Ash (Ian Holm) – the most level-featured, impassive of the crew – tells Dallas, 'Mother wants to talk to you.' He has an instinct half a beat quicker than Dallas's – or is he simply that much more attuned to Mother? Ash is prim, crisply dressed (no one else is really tidy or uniformed), precise and just a little prissy.

Dallas – he is Captain Dallas in the credits – wanders away with his mug of coffee. The Texan name does maybe add to his possible attractiveness in Ripley's eyes. But 'Captain Dallas' in 1979 is also a year or so into *Dallas* on TV, enough to give the name an undertone of bogusness. He moves away from the crew to a private antechamber, where he takes the steps – ones only a captain knows, it seems – to gain entrance to a sand-coloured chamber where lights sparkle. This is the centre of the ship's computer, Mother's home, and Dallas taps into the system to discover why he has been called.

We cut back to the ship under way, being 'piloted' by Ash, Kane, Lambert and Ripley – but does it really need piloting, or is it, so to speak, like a movie, propelled by its own narrative plan? They suppose they are coming close to Earth, but the data on their screens is unfamiliar. 'It's not our system,' says Ripley. There are close-ups of the four of them (we never have a master shot to show how they are arranged), their faces illuminated by screens, the curve of their heads duplicated by lavaliere microphones. They don't know where they are. Ripley tries to radio to Earth, to the Antarctica station. Nothing. Then Lambert (the navigator?) realises they are in a quite different galaxy, nowhere near home yet.

We cut away again to Parker and Brett, white-clad figures in the dark lower corridors of the *Nostromo* – somewhere close to the engine room perhaps, grumbling together about their inferior status.

Then we cut back to the flight deck, as Parker and Brett and Dallas arrive at the same time. Parker enjoys telling Ash he's sitting in his seat, and when the punctilious Ash gets up Parker sweeps the seat clear with his hand – does Ash actually leave a fine residue?

Dallas tells them they're not home yet. Mother has interrupted their journey, and woken them up, so as to check out a signal it has picked up from this other galaxy – an acoustical beacon at 12-second intervals. Parker argues that theirs is a commercial ship, not a rescue ship – though he'd go along for a better share. But Ash reminds him that the contract – we believe that Ash knows that document by heart – requires that any signal, any intelligent signal, be investigated, or all shares are to be abandoned. Parker argues. But Dallas snaps at him – the commander, at last – 'Listen to the man!' And Parker has to concede, while Brett grins in that drooping, enervated way Harry Dean Stanton has, as if to say, We're the suckers again. They are going in to the planet where the signal is coming from, every twelve seconds.

4

There are systems for this crew, rules, and a Mother to guide them. But it's striking that they are so undisciplined, so garrulous, so informal – it's another sign that the ship doesn't quite require them or their strict attention. And that has only added to their tone of grievance, their boredom. There will never be any hint of their place in the Company that employs them, or its command; of what they are paid or why they serve. There is no marked evidence of their skill, their courage or their determination. They seem to be examples of some advanced, futuristic state – an age of high technology – in which human capacity or imagination has been dulled or neutralised. They seem to have no families at home, and no special ties to each other. They are not bright or alert people; they are sleepy. They are not quite like us – are they?

5

'Going in' on this seemingly desolate planet (I'm not sure it's even called that, but I hardly know how else to name it) involves the *Nostromo* releasing its shuttle, or landing module. All of the crew go in that shuttle, which seemed odd even in 1979. Of course, the *Nostromo* can remain in its orbit without custodians, but isn't it unnecessarily reckless to send all seven down to the surface? The answer would have to be 'yes' in all circumstances save one – that only one of these seven is meant to survive. It might require an unusually analytical viewer to make that deduction so early – yet, grant the premise, and notice the more intriguing question: which of the seven will it be who survives? Dallas, because he is skipper? Kane, because he woke first? Parker, because he is such a 'character'? Brett, because he might be a comic? Lambert, because she's the least likely? Ash, because he seems so aware? Ripley, because she is Sigourney Weaver? Yet no one then in the wide world knew who Weaver was, and Ripley has done very little in the movie except behave herself.

Still, she warns 'Turbulence' in advance as the shuttle settles. We see schematics of the surface on the shuttle controls; we have shots of the shuttle itself, gingerly edging into the uneven air. There is a bump, a small fire, and some damage to the craft. Dallas is deeply depressed by the incident – it is an odd, disconcerting reaction, as if to suggest how unsuited he is to command. Or how fatigued. Brett and Parker examine the damage, and will have to repair it. Tell them seventeen hours, Brett suggests, and then he gives his sly grin when Parker tells Dallas twenty-five hours over the intercom.

The shuttle has sensors that can measure the environment of the new planet. Ash rhapsodises over it, a little like Sir Anthony Blunt with a rare Poussin. The surface is rock and lava, with a lot of coal deep down, or 'below the line'. As for the atmosphere, it is not breathable, of course, but Ash revels in its harsh composition. The beacon that has drawn them is about two thousand yards away. A comfortable walk, Dallas suggests in his surly way, and Ash gives a modest smile as if to say it's not really for him to make that call. In all this interplay there is a steady build-up in Ash's drab authority – the more clearly he is in the know, the more impersonal he becomes.

Dallas orders Kane and Lambert to make the walk with him towards the beacon. And so they put on their spacesuits, always a depressing moment in an interesting sci-fi film, for just as spacesuits restrict our view of a face, so they tend to mask any uniqueness of human movement or gesture. What I'm trying to say is that, with the best will in the world, the slow trudge across broken ground to the beacon is one of those necessary, tension-stretching doldrums in a film. The pseudo-moonlit planet looks fetching; the music is atmospheric; but the journey is so much less than the getting there. Still, it is important to remind ourselves that when we first saw *Alien* we had no idea where its threat would come from. And so, ostensibly, the three hikers are in danger on what looks and feels like a dark and stormy night – the already tedious Lambert complains that she can't see a thing.

But as they make their way, fascinating things happen on the shuttle. There is a bantering encounter in the hold between Parker and Brett and Ripley. The two guys bring up the matter of their share again. She says they'll get what they deserve, never fear. There is some sexual innuendo in the air. Flickering lights and steam intrude on the close-up of Ripley – she has never looked more romantic. In humour, she tells them to fuck off – and if they have any trouble, she'll be on the bridge. It's as if sex in this world has to be underground. (Can there be erections in a weightless state?)

Meanwhile, Ash makes it his duty to watch the three searchers. And so he sits, alone, in a kind of viewing hatch – he is seen from the rear, and the shot has a certain wistful splendour. It makes him seem more in charge than he ought to be. At the same time – having asked Ash first – Ripley begins to run the beacon signal through computer analysis. Immense patterns of 1s and 0s appear on her screen; and we see close-ups of Ripley's scrutiny in which every such shot makes her more impressive. As she gazes at the screen, there is a cut to Jones the cat, licking its lips.

Then, in a matter-of-fact observation, Ripley tells Ash that Mother is suggesting this beacon might be more of a warning than an S.O.S. This is one of the great, delicate moments in the film, and it depends on the principle of intellectual discrimination, as opposed to demonstration. We do not see what Mother or Ripley means. We merely note the way in which one apparently benign or open thing – a close-up, say – may mean something much more than its first impression.

6

But between Ripley's off-handed urge to examine the signal and her uncertain realisation, much more has happened, enough for us to suspect her finding is correct. The three walkers on the planet come to an extraordinary . . . ruin or monument?

'Ash, can you see this?' Dallas asks. For the explorers have television cameras that are transmitting back to Ash in the viewing shell. 'Yes,' he replies, 'I've never seen anything like it.' There is reverence in his voice and his pale grey eyes. And so there should be.

Prostrate on the ground, or growing out of it, is a very large two-pronged form, the prongs like limbs or phalluses reaching for each other. Nothing here exists as is, but in terms of resemblance or metaphor. Are we seeing some kind of space vehicle that has crashed? A castle that has sunk into the ground? Or is it the shell of a creature? Might it even be an absurd, defiant, inexplicable construction or creation, something that is quite simply there, beyond all reason or purpose?

It is reptilian, in that its ribbed surface is hardened. It is sometimes like sinew, muscle, bone and the leathery skin that contains physique. There are places where the bold upthrust shapes seem like saddle pommels, like the stock and barrel of guns, triggers, bolts. And others where it reminds us of body parts, intimate recesses, sexual geography. And everything seems to be made or cast in some hard, black rubber. The form could be a dead, hollowed animal, and there are moments when the explorers seem to be inside the cavernous interior of a whale. Simultaneously, it seems both ancient and very new, dead yet coiled or poised.

This creation, this set, this phenomenon, is the work of H. R. Giger, and it is one of the great sets in film history, not just infinite in its possibilities or meanings, but an emphatic assertion of some strange culture that made it and put intonations of design, order, intelligence and magic in it. For it is suggestive and frightening, too, and it is the first moment in all the *Alien* movies in which the ambiguities of the body are introduced as subject matter. After all, if it is so beautiful, so brimming with art or meaning, is this 'body' alive or dead?

Our view of the 'body' comes in two ways – the breaking up TV footage beamed back to the shuttle; and an absolutely lucid, magisterial coverage from on high, which is far more than the explorers could see or experience. This observance, in other words, is removed from the minds of the humans. (We do hear the awed Lambert say, 'Let's get out of here' – she's worried enough to feel the menace.) It is a grave, visual description that subtly celebrates the . . . shrine, the holy place, the site of fascination.

At one point, Dallas comes upon a clear reptilian figure – a fossil, a frozen thing, or a depiction – and as he moves away from it the camera lingers, letting us register an eye and a mouth, the husk of Evil. This is the first glimpse of anything like a monster, yet no character sees it – rather, the film shows it to *us* and says, look, in the spirit that would share wonders with us.

That's when Ripley tells Ash that maybe the signal is a warning. She wants to go out there and tell, or get, the others.

'What's the point?' asks Ash. There is anguish in his voice, as if loveliness might be stepped on. 'I mean, by the time it took to get there, they'll have found out if it's a warning or not. Yes?' This is the first real speech in the film, the longest, so irrational yet so begging that Ash's little boy nature slots into 'Mother' like a bullet going into the breach.

7

Ian Holm was then forty-seven; his given name was Ian Holm Cuthbert, and he had been born in Goodmayes, a village in England.

He had seemed an outstandingly promising actor on the British stage and on television in the late 'fifties and early 'sixties. He had had a romantic quality and the darkness of great villains – he had been a very notable Richard III for the Royal Shakespeare Company. But he was not tall; and the hair did not grow violently all over his head. He had supporting parts in several films from the late 'sixties onwards. He played a tight-lipped King John in *Robin and Marian*, he was established as a character actor, and a few years later he would be nominated for Best Supporting Actor as the Italian trainer in *Chariots of Fire*. It was not until the 1990s, with a Lear on the London stage and such movies as *Night Falls on Manhattan* and *The Sweet Hereafter*, that he was plainly perceived as a great actor, worthy of entire films.

No one knew that yet in 1979, and Holm's Englishness set him apart a little in the essentially American crew of the *Nostromo*. (Yes, John Hurt is English, too – and, of course, the movie was shot in England.) But Holm's Englishness here is an ingredient in the slightly querulous side to Ash's character – to say nothing of his potential for the sinister, a quality that Americans frequently trust to English actors.* The great line examined on page 28 is said with an aloof English accent – and so it seems extra-neurotic in the American spaceman idiom of the crew. (Astronauts then spoke a dry, clipped language designed for effective radio communications. They rarely talked personally, or impulsively. But Holm's long line is so needy, so vulnerable, and also so dotty.) It makes him the largest person in the movie so far – but how can that be when he is so short, so un-American, so nerdy, so quietly menacing? Without knowing it, the series is looking far ahead; for one day, one age, it would have an inhuman as its hero and engine.

---

*From Basil Rathbone, Claude Rains, Charles Laughton and George Sanders to Anthony Hopkins as Hannibal Lecter, English eloquence promises wickedness in the American imagination.

8

The film doesn't give Ripley time or opportunity to respond to Ash's downplaying of her discovery. Yet there could be that instant in which she feels rebuked or dismissed; just as, in hindsight, the film might play more richly if she was harassed or unsettled by the sexual overtures from Parker and Brett. Sigourney Weaver would say that she always tried to play her character 'as a soldier', and it's reasonable to suppose that Ripley has been toughened by service. On the other hand, if the action is so constructed that she will emerge as heroine and life-force, then it would do no harm to have her a little more innocent or less worldly at the outset. One extra layer of shyness would have helped – a crushed glance in reaction to Ash's grandmotherly intimidation.

No matter, we must go back to the great shell of being out there on the planet's surface. For contact is about to be made. We see Kane's face, within his helmet, gazing in wonder at the spectacle. He has gone deeper into the being than the others. Indeed, he is lowered on a hawser down into the hold or bowels of the being – he calls it a cave, 'hot as the tropics'. Then he discovers several rows of what he describes as eggs – though they are not much smaller than those baskets or jars in which the forty thieves once hid. Kane's face – the face that woke first, the agonised, aged boy's face that John Hurt possesses, the face that feels dead – registers the marvel.

One egg peels back at the top. Something like a pink brain or sac can be seen within, moist, fresh, veined – is it even pulsing? Like a placenta? And Kane shines a light on the outer texture of the egg so that we can see, within, a moving embryo – evidently reptilian, like a small dinosaur or a pterodactyl. It is, let's say, no larger than Jones, but even in this strange, amateurish X-ray, it seems prickly, tailed and with teeth.

Kane applies a probe, gently, to the pink mass, and like a whip, the arm and claw of something cruel lashes out of the egg and grips the front of his helmet. This happens too swiftly for us to see accurately, but the aggressive limb is scaled, sinewed, with claws or fingers, and its impact, or shock, is enough to render Kane unconscious. This is the first great gotcha! of the film; and the first bodily seizure of the series. It leaves us wondering how long, in the vast maw of drifting space, that leaping clamp had been waiting just to get someone.

We cut to a long shot of the surface of the planet. The shape of the being is vaguely apparent through the mist. A great wind is blowing. There is a shot of Ash reclining in his chair, waiting, not so much unaware as patient. And then we cut back to the outside and see two spacesuits carrying a third – like polar explorers struggling in a blizzard to bring a wounded man into camp.

Dallas calls Ripley to be sure she is there – that does help establish the point that, in his absence, she is in charge. But, already, Ash is hurrying to the interlock hatch. Over the radio, Dallas says they have to get Kane to the infirmary. There is then a full close-up of Ripley, as seen from three-quarters on, and a little low; her skin tone is warm and blooming. Ripley purses her mouth in indications of thought. She mentions the 24-hour quarantine rules, the need not to bring any questionable element into the ship. He could die, is all Dallas can answer. And the close-up of Ripley again, sombre but secure: 'No, I can't do that. And if you were in my position you'd do the same.'

Is this going to be a Kane mutiny? Is Ripley being officious or properly firm? Is she the most natural leader in the crew? Ash settles everything by just opening the hatch.

9

We have passed over an implausibility. I mention it not to be fussy or troublesome, only to show how far inconsistencies or 'errors' are best evaded when they are magical and central. To be precise, on the surface of the desolate planet there is a visible chill – I called it polar, and that is what the imagery suggests. Yet in the 'cave' of the being there is that warmth that Kane calls 'as hot as the tropics'. (There is something Conradian in that remark, as befits a crewman on the *Nostromo*.★) The heat is there to protect the embryos and their fertilisation. It is heat to fill a very large chamber – yet there is no hint of source or generation, and nothing that has been picked up by the *Nostromo*'s sophisticated sensor devices. In other words, this heat is a given – like enough light in the cave for us to see the details of Giger's design. And both heat and light are the manifestations of some enormous, unexplained intelligence – the subject over which the *Alien* films have such mixed feelings. (Do we run the risk in pursuing our own intelligent programme of evolving into creatures or forces we find . . . alien? Or at least as alien as the naked ape?) Very well, but let us notice how far in all cinema, light (at least) and the sense of some intricate machinery hovers out there, benignly. We have to hope so. Yet we are by now used to being horrified, too.

10

Ash's insubordination (or initiative) is passed over. We go straight to a shot of a fine tool (it is probably just a blade, but don't rule out laser assistance) that is gingerly cutting away the glass or perspex or plastic of Kane's helmet. For something bizarre occurred as they carried Kane back to the shuttle. The creature has somehow penetrated the helmet and become attached to Kane's very face. As the two halves of severed helmet are peeled back, we see that the creature is on the face like a great, possessive gas mask. This is the claw or the hand – there are fingers reaching around the head, through his hair – but there is a pulsing sac above the claw, and a long reptilian tail that is wound not once, but twice, around Kane's throat.

★Conrad is one of those authors much referred to by film-makers (if not always read), perhaps because he is such a visionary of large, human enterprises that go astray, or which founder on the vanities of men.

Kane is in the infirmary; Dallas and Ash are standing over him, ready for surgery if they can decide on a procedure. The other crew members are in a gallery, watching through the window. Dallas is for taking action: it is hardly clear that Kane can breathe. But he sees that the creature's grip (and its will is already perceptible) might result in its tearing Kane's face off in an attempt at removal. Ash is for doing nothing. Parker, outside, says why not freeze Kane's body?

They put Kane in some kind of scanner (the beauty of science fiction is taking such things for granted). The 'M.R.I.' (Multiple Resonance Image) shows that the creature is down Kane's throat, and seems to be giving him oxygen: the intrusion of one body on another is one of the more ambiguous motifs in the *Alien* pictures – for sometimes deadly attack (or rape) also sustains, as in strange, unwanted pregnancies. There is even an allusion to coupling, or love-making, as a kind of threat – hence the series' very guarded view of sex.

Ash advises against being hasty. If the creature is giving Kane oxygen, then removal might kill the astronaut. Dallas is cowboy enough to insist on action – cut it off, he says. Ash makes it plain that he is not taking responsibility, but he cuts at the knuckle on one of the fingers on Kane's head – these fingers are like lobster legs. There is a hiss and a milky yellow liquid emerges, falling on the infirmary floor, and burning it away.

In a moment, the residue has gone through two storeys in the structure of the shuttle. The creature's blood, it seems, is acid of a very potent kind. Some defence mechanism, says Parker; you don't dare kill it. There is also a bit of business with a pen belonging to Brett, thrust into the last acid, and seen to smoulder and smoke. Harry Dean Stanton looks at it like a primitive who has never encountered fire before.

There is a cut and a short time-lapse. We see Parker and Brett trying to repair the shuttle. Whatever they have attempted, it does not work. Parker says they should never have landed in the first place.

Then we are in the airy, white light of the infirmary. Kane is on the bed, the creature still clamped to his face. The camera prowls around the place, as if alone there. But then it finds Ash working at some television X-ray coverage of Kane. Ripley appears; she has slipped into the room; she may even have been the prowling personality in the camera. She asks Ash about Kane, and 'our guest'. Ash is uneasy, defensive; he says that the creature seems to have a special resistance to adverse environmental conditions – 'a tough little son of a bitch'.

'And you let him in,' says Ripley. She is quiet, but looking to pick a fight. Ash says he simply forgot her superior position. 'You also forgot the scientific division's own quarantine laws,' she argues. 'No,' says Ash, 'I didn't forget that. It was a risk I was willing to take.' Ripley stands now as true officer material, ready to sacrifice Kane, determined to observe the overall security, and instinctively hostile to Ash's claims for science.

Alien and its successors are sci-fi films that grow to loathe and fear science. 'You do your job,' says Ash, 'and let me do mine, yes?' But Ripley's sceptical gaze tells us that she does not trust that kind of compartmentalisation.

After all, one cut knuckle ate away the structure of two levels in the shuttle. And now the creature is embracing Kane in a way that exceeds all kinds of love, even that of a mother.

11

Sigourney Weaver would be twenty-nine when *Alien* opened, but it was her first real part in a picture. She had had a moment in *Annie Hall* previously, and a significant role in an Israeli picture, *Madman*, which had scarcely been seen – Weaver was very sympathetic to Israel, and had worked briefly on a kibbutz. But she was quite evidently WASP: the daughter of Pat Weaver, the president of NBC, the man who created the *Today* and *Tonight* shows, and of Elizabeth Inglis, an English actress who had had small parts in *The 39 Steps* for Hitchcock, and *The Letter* for Wyler. The child had been raised in grand homes, often full of show-business people.

At the age of fourteen, Susan Weaver took the decision to call herself 'Sigourney' Weaver – it was a name used in *The Great Gatsby*, and she felt it was better suited to the considerable height that already seemed her destiny. She would reach 5 ft 10½ in; and she would live with the knowledge that her height intimidated many small-minded producers – to say nothing of men in general.

She entered Stanford, where she was an anti-war protester, an explorer in student theatre, and eventually a B.A. in English. Then she went to the Yale Drama School where she was a contemporary of John Guare, Wendy Wasserstein and Christopher Durang. Her education, and thus her mind, are way beyond those of most actresses – Meryl Streep, who went to Vassar and Yale, is Weaver's closest comparison. That led her into plays written by Guare and Durang and an understudy role in Sir John Gielgud's production of *The Constant Wife*, which starred Ingrid Bergman, another lofty actress.

So she was cast in the movie as an 'unknown', but she was never reticent or demure. Not only tall, she was earnest, confident and visibly smart. Yet she had an unaffected youthfulness, too, a kind of no-nonsense innocence. And, for a tall woman, she was not just undaunted, but serene and graceful in her movements. All those things, I think, are observable early in the film. What no one could guess at was a depth of character, a decency, that would prove vital in letting the story run to four parts over nearly twenty years.

12

Ash wins the battle of wills with Ripley. Her amber-hued face looks away from him and she retreats. Ash takes a gulp from a beaker of what seems like milk, but it could be bicarbonate of soda or some other non-toxic lubricant. We hardly expect fresh milk on this *Nostromo*.

But the next cut takes us to a distant view of the shuttle, its inner lights not just burning but vaguely Christmassy, as we hear the far-off strains of Mozart's *Eine kleine Nachtmusik*, and a close-up of Dallas, reclining, leaning into the music – a skipper who needs to get away and find some consolation, the artistic loner on the ship.

His reverie is interrupted by Ash on the intercom: 'I think you should have a look at Kane.' Dallas is a little irritated, but he turns off the music and calls Ripley to meet him in the infirmary.

There is then, suddenly, a big close-up – his head prostrate – of Kane, his face clear except for what may be the drops and rivulets of tears or sweat. The creature has gone – evidently of its own accord.

Dallas, Ash and Ripley enter the infirmary, the two men in white, the woman in grey. A long shot poses their cautious procedure in the hatchway, and Ripley is the tallest of the three, yet as limber as a basketball player. There's not a hint of awkwardness in her height.

The camera is at floor level to show their hesitant exploration of the infirmary, for they suppose the creature is somewhere. Ripley looks under the bed. Ash uses a probe to feel in corners of the room. And then, as Ripley looks down at Kane, the metal flex of some power supply over the bed is mimicked by a tentacle reaching out for Ripley's hair as the remains of the creature drop on her. Not that we are sure it is dead. After all, if the creature had gone into the overhead to die, hadn't it found a secure place? And if it falls now, is it chance that it picks on Ripley – or a way of identifying her as its best opponent?

Ash pokes a prod into the soft underside of the creature. It tenses, but he says it's only a reflex action.

On a cut, we see that softness – like a large oyster – spread out as a specimen. Yet note, the film does not reveal the entire monster – we do not see exactly how long the tail was. The partial views of the creature will help endow it with a dynamic for startling change. Indeed, this monster does prove to possess amazing powers of growth, beyond our normal sense of organic life* – it is as if the monster

*Dan O'Bannon had once had the notion that the alien could adapt to imitate its various victims.

expands in response to the emotional impact it has on people. As it becomes more frightening, so it threatens infinity.

There is a very beautiful shot, the frame filled with the three heads of Dallas, Ash and Ripley, in a line and all in effective focus, looking at the folds and flaps of soft flesh. Ripley wants to get rid of it – void it in any way possible. Ash despairs of her. He tut-tuts; 'Ripley, for God's sake,' he begins. This is a creature such as science has never met: it has to go back. (That need is expressed very early in this first film.) Ripley protests. The decision goes to Dallas, in so many ways the weakest (the most Mozart-needy) of the three. 'It's your decision, Ash,' he sighs. 'You're the science officer.'

Whereupon Dallas walks away, hounded by Ripley. He will not stop and face her, so she has the wit to close a hatchway ahead of him. He turns wearily to face her. 'Look, I just run the ship!' he says, abdicating all 'scientific' matters to Ash. Since when does that happen? she asks.

'It happens, my dear,' – this is surely the gesture of condescension more than an allusion to real closeness – 'because that's the way the Company wants it to happen.'

The *Nostromo*, apparently, is not a national vessel; it is part of the Company fleet. We cannot tell whether this implies a time in which companies have surpassed nations, or are in parallel with them. Nor is it clear how far this Company is a subtle merger of commercial interests with that other notorious, company, the C.I.A. But it is the first note of hierarchy in this period of history, and it is a sign of authority so great that even a ship's skipper is resigned to not being completely in charge.

Is that standard procedure, she asks – can she be such a novice, or is Ripley just asking the dumb question we need to have answered?

'Standard procedure,' he says – and Dallas's anger now explains his lassitude and even the way he slurs his lines – 'is to do what the hell they tell you to do.' (One wonders whether this use of 'hell' isn't just a nostalgic affectation, a sign of Dallas being a throwback.)

Ripley asks Dallas if he has ever shipped out with Ash before – a question that surely tells us she has never worked with him in the past. He admits that five times he worked with another science officer, and then two days before this departure that man was replaced with Ash.★

'I don't trust him,' says Ripley.

'I don't trust anyone,' he answers, and then he changes the subject by asking about the state of repairs. Not yet, she says, but he nags at her and finds that in fact the ship could leave. He pulls rank on her and rebukes her for not keeping him informed. 'I just want to get the hell out of here,' says Dallas.

On a cut, the shuttle lifts off. The engines rumble. The craft shakes. There is a perfunctory sense of danger and difficulty. But it passes. Parker cries out in elation, 'Walk in the park!' And the next thing we see is the entire *Nostromo* advancing through dark space.

13

We are on the ship, homeward bound. The group are together again, and we fix on Brett who is rolling cigarettes. Talking of Kane, Parker reckons they should freeze him. 'Right,' says Brett. Ripley remarks on the way Brett says 'Right' to everything. He pauses a beat and says 'Right' again. The banter is edging into a row when Lambert appears and gives Dallas the news that their trip home has another ten months to go. They are all set back

---

★What does that mean? That the *Nostromo*'s mission was never all those tons of ore, but always this diversion on the way home?

by this news – does it mean more of the 'sleep' we saw at the beginning?

Then the intercom buzzer sounds. Ripley picks it up and says 'Yes'. But Ash's voice says, 'Dallas, you should come and see Kane.' They all make ready to leave for the infirmary, and Brett closes the scene with another 'Right'.

We cut to the face of Kane, conscious and awake again, but turning his neck as if it were stiff. He's drinking a lot of water, and doesn't remember more than just some 'horrible dream about smothering'. They laugh and make ready to rejoice at having him back. Brett mentions the 'old freezerino' – is that their sleep? and it's agreed that they'll have a feast before 'turning in'.

Cut to the meal table, where Kane is piling his plate with a kind of pasta. There is an air of camaraderie. But Ash is watching Kane with dispassionate curiosity. A string of spaghetti dangles from Kane's mouth. He starts to cough.

You know what is coming – it is at least nineteen years after the first movie was released. But in 1979, no one could be sure, or escape seeing *it* for the first time. Kane is seized by coughing. The others lay him on the table. They put the handle of a spoon in his mouth to prevent choking. His white T-shirt seems to be straining.

Then something beneath the fabric breaks, and there is a ragged circle of blood on the shirt. Seconds later, the snout of the monster breaks clear – it is a yellowy, blunt, snake-like head, though without eyes. It looks round and we see its tail stirring, thrashing in the blood. Lambert is covered in the red spray.

The monster is an infant, yet it has heavy steel teeth. And when it opens its jaws to cry out, the sound is very young, yet harsh and fearsome. And with that sound, the monster scuttles away from the body that has given it birth, from the table, and into the dark recesses of the *Nostromo*. The scene ends on Ash's face, like a believer who has seen a saint, but who finds the image more beautiful and more terrifying than he ever fancied.

14

This monster is not as terrible as its way of coming. Its head and body seem about the size of a forearm, its head like a fist. Parker makes to lash at it with a table knife, and he might have dispatched it, but Ash, of course, says don't touch. The most daring thing about this monster is its childlike air – not just the cry and the eager looking around, but its being still wreathed in blood.

What made audiences scream in 1979, what had some people vomiting as they ran away, was the eruption from within. For I think very few people then foresaw that the monster was going to demand birth from Kane's body. We had never seen one body breaking out of another, even if there had been hints of that in *The Exorcist*. We had not really understood the title, *Alien*, until this scene, and the absolute, parasitic subduing of one organism by another. We did not know, and had not yet acquired, that metaphoric sense of invasive illness that has been conveyed by AIDS. Cancer was the most evident root of the metaphor. Even so, the body seemed more secure then. And the nausea, the gulping and retching, came in the sudden upheaval of understanding, of what had been done down Kane's throat. For the man had been made pregnant.

And as it happened, we would never see that infant monster again, anyway. It was just a step in time and evolution.

15

There is a slow pan shot of empty corridors on the *Nostromo* before we come to a gathering of what we may call the 'survivors'. They await the funeral, or the voiding, of Kane. We see into a sealed chamber – it has an Egyptian aura – and the corpse swathed in white. There is no argument. Ash does not ask to have this body frozen so that some later inquiry can see how it became host to the monster. 'Anyone want to say anything?' Dallas asks gruffly – clearly he is abdicating. The heroic American movie had seldom declined that offer – even if it was the blunt matter of John Wayne reading words over someone he had had to kill. There is no mention of Kane's family, not so much as a rosebud of observance. The switch is hit, and the white pellet goes end over end into space, like a cigarette end tossed away in the night. Life for the *Nostromo* crew is all a matter of being awake *now*; the past, and history, are gone – as if narcotised.

A little later, on the ship, the six are planning their campaign. Brett has made a prod that carries an electric charge. Ash has fashioned a tracking device that responds to 'micro-changes in air density'. He admits that its range is not great (Ripley will speak of five metres – but later still it seems to carry much further.)

Dallas picks two teams: himself, with Ash and Lambert; Ripley, with Parker and Brett. He orders no heroics – especially from Parker – just track the thing down, catch it, and put it in an airlock.

There is a cut, and then we are with Ripley's party, in a part of the ship where the lighting system has failed. Parker does what he can with it, and the lights come back on.

'We gotta stick together,' says Ripley, a sentiment that clashes oddly with what will happen. Then her tracking device registers something beyond a door. The three of them stand by it. Parker and Brett hold a heavy rope net. The door slides open, and there is a big close-up of a trapped cat – Jones – as fearsome in tooth, claw and hissing as any monster. (We may recall *The Incredible Shrinking Man*, who was hunted by his own cat.)

The cat escapes their clumsy and very nervous efforts. And Brett is sent to pursue Jones – the very opposite of Ripley's recent instinct. It is a silly contradiction, noted by several reviewers, and one that helps us see the weaknesses in this section of the story. For in truth, or in drama, there are now only three vital forces on the *Nostromo* – Ripley, the creature, and Ash. There will be an inevitable final confrontation, and four people who have to be removed first (Parker, Brett, Lambert, Dallas). The film does not surpass that predictability, and does not really have a master-stroke for handling it.

And so there is a brief passage, or soliloquy, for the lugubrious Harry Dean Stanton, as the rather inept Brett wanders off into the shadowy interior of the ship calling 'Kitty . . . kitty' in his forlorn way. There is a fine, low-angle shot of Brett's gaunt face, the wide, empty eyes and the general air of a doomed zombie. He comes close to the cat again, but it evades him – we may ask ourselves whether such voyages were ever permitted to carry cats; or was Jones smuggled on board?

Then Brett finds something on the floor. It looks a little like a discarded Victorian corset, but it is the abandoned skin of the creature, enough to suggest that it is developing.

Brett follows the cat (there is a tiny hint of Alice's adventures) into the next chamber, and we discover it is the floor of a soaring vault – a cooling tower. Heavy chains swing in the air, and we hear the fine rain of condensation. The shadow of a chain is seen behind Brett, teasingly suggestive of a monstrous limb. He stands in the rain, looks up, takes off his cap, and lets the moisture wash down on his unshaven face. There is a perilous sense of peace or cleansing, though we feel how vulnerable and off-guard Brett is. And we wonder, does he come here often during the voyage to recall the Earth's gentle rain? Or is the rain bitter, toxic even, the drool of a beast?

We see the cat, in a doorway, hiding. Brett hears it and moves forward. We see his face, gazing at the cat, calling to it. But Jones flinches. We see a large coil move behind Brett – a limb – so much larger than that prior, rampant infant. Then we see the head of the monster, sideways on, dripping with the glue-like saliva it has. Nothing in the shot gives an exact sense of size, but this monster looms over Brett. He turns to face it. We see the cruel jaws open, the teeth as big as tines on a rake.

The creature strikes. There is a glimpse, too quick to register, of Brett, pierced and bloodied. We hear his helpless screams and see the face of Jones, looking up, as if Brett had been hoisted up to hang amid the chains, like meat.

Some sort of time-lapse occurs. We come to a huge close-up of

Parker, who has found the body of his friend, Brett. 'Whatever it was, it was big.' And a moment later he says, 'It's huge – like a man.'

Dallas reasons that the monster, having now taken to the airshafts, may be trapped in that system. But someone will have to go into those cramped tunnels to find it. Ripley rides Ash: 'What can Science do to help?' He is irritated, but he says why not use fire, most creatures are afraid of fire. Parker agrees to rig up some home-made incendiary units.

We have a view from outside of the *Nostromo* passing through space.

Then Dallas is alone in the computer room with Mother. He is trying to seek any guidance about dealing with the monster, but the machine says it is 'unable to compute'. He asks what his chances are and the answer comes back in lime-green letters on the screen: 'DOES NOT COMPUTE.' The skipper leans forward over his console in reflection: this last possible male hero is close to stricken. But the question remains, why is Mother so unhelpful?

Well, Dallas goes into the ventilation system, carrying a light and the flame-thrower Parker has made. They are octagonal corridors again, so small he has to crouch, breathing heavily. As he moves, he orders the hatches closed behind him – they are like the irises in cameras.

Lambert has the tracking system with the bright dot of Dallas on it – yet surely she is much more than five metres away? He explores, he tests out stretches of corridor with bursts of flame-thrower. And then Lambert picks up another dot, coming towards him. She panics. We have Ripley's face, gorgeous in a big close-up, on the radio system, so much calmer and more attentive – yet anxious, too.

Dallas can't make out where the creature is, though their dots are converging. He feels slime on the floor, the spoor of the beast. He goes down a staircase, turns with his light, and there it is – like a kid playing 'Boo!' at Halloween, two hands raised; and in the split second

that we see it, is there even a grin on the wicked face? The picture
cuts out, like a lost TV signal.

16

Then there were four: Ripley, Ash, Lambert and Parker, with
Ripley in charge. As Dallas scrambled in the ventilators, there was
one profile close-up of Ash, not so much unconcerned as reflecting
like a connoisseur on how this beast functions. 'DOES NOT COMPUTE'
suddenly seems like a kindness, a way of not telling the sucker in Las
Vegas that the house is the sure bet.

The flame-thrower Dallas carried is slammed down on a table.
Parker says it was the only thing left – 'No blood, no Dallas,
nothing.'* Parker wants to kill the beast. A weepy Lambert is for
destroying the ship and escaping on the shuttle. But it won't hold
four, argues Ripley. 'Unless anyone has a better idea,' she says – and
Ash is behind her, out of focus, as she speaks – they'll keep to Dallas's
plan. Go in again, find it 'and blow the fucker out into space'.

Then Ripley turns on Ash, who studiously keeps his back to her.
Has he any advice? No, he says, he's 'still collating'. Ripley laughs in
a mixture of scorn and desperation, and says that nothing is what he
has done all along. But now she can talk to Mother herself. Ash gives
her a dry, mocking salute – he is photographed more and more from
odd angles, in cut-off close-ups with never a 'normal' straight view.

Ripley enters the computer room, her eyes wide open where
Dallas's were resigned slits. She asks why Science has been unable
to deal with the alien. 'UNABLE TO CLARIFY' she is told. But she
hammers in more requests until she finds an order 937 – for the
Science Officer's eyes only – the gist of which was a rerouting of
the *Nostromo*, to gather a specimen, all other concerns dispensed with,
'CREW EXPENDABLE'.

---

*They shot a scene of Dallas imprisoned in the alien's cocoon, but then cut it.

From a side-on point of view, Ripley's head – her mane of curly hair – rocks back in disgust, and there is Ash beside and behind her, having slipped silently into the room.

In a rage, she grabs him and throws him against the wall. He seems shocked, or damaged, and slides along the wall. She leaves, to tell the others, but as she advances Ash closes the hatches ahead of her. She is irked; she turns back to him. She sees a trickle of white liquid on his temple. We realise that her nose is bloody from their scuffle.

Then he lunges, awkwardly, and tears at her hair. He throws her down; although he seems stricken, he has unexpected strength. She is semi-conscious on the floor. He rolls up a magazine – it seems like a girlie magazine – with the intent of forcing it into her mouth. She comes to. They struggle. Parker and Lambert appear and Parker tries to pull Ash off Ripley. But Ash puts a hand, or a claw, on Parker's chest, and the big man screams at the surprising pain.

Then Parker hits Ash in the back of the neck with a heavy piece of metal. Ash spins round the room, his mouth frothing with white liquid, his hands fluttering. He is not so much out of control as sent into some ultimate spasmodic behaviour.

Then Parker knocks Ash's head right off – nothing but wiring now connects the head and its flap of throat to the body. Yet Ash fights still, even with his head hanging down his back, even with his white fluid flying all over the room. Until Lambert hits him with the electronic prod.

The robot is wrecked. But Ripley and Parker can do an emergency job on his wiring so that the severed head will respond. Ash jerks back from nullity to 'on' again; white ooze drools from his lips; his voice is tinny and unclear. He says his special order, 937, was to bring the alien life form back to Earth.

'Damned Company!' seethes Parker.

Ripley asks the head how they can kill the alien.

Ian Holm, now, rises to his greatest moment in the film, not just robotic but a defective robot. 'You can't,' he tells her. 'It's a perfect organism, its structural perfection is matched only by its hostility.'

Lambert sees the bizarre kinship. 'You admire it,' she says.

Ash admits he admires the purity, the absence of conscience or considerations of morality. It is in his performance, here, that we detect the possible soul of a machine, the desire for the new level of life to be recognised, or appreciated. Ash is alien, too, but oddly touching.

Ripley is about to cut him off for all time, but he intervenes:

'Last word. I can't lie to you about your chances. But' – and a grin, a smirk, that old dislike of Ripley, has its moment – 'you have my sympathies.'

Savagely, she pulls his plug.

17

'We're going to blow up the ship,' says Ripley. She, Parker and Lambert will then have to make their escape in the shuttle. As the trio pull themselves together, Parker turns his flame-thrower on Ash's discarded head. In two bursts, we see the 'skin' come off like thick paint, exposing the hard plastic skull.

The switches that will explode the ship leave a ten-minute running time. Ripley tells the others to search for as much coolant as possible – the shuttle will depend on it. So Parker and Lambert set off on that mission, while Ripley begins to prepare the shuttle for its separate flight.

No, it's not the way I'd do it, either. Every lesson of the movie so far is 'stick together', which Ripley has stressed time and again. And don't ask why the coolant is so vital. Just accept that sooner or later this game is meant to be one on one.

Even so, as Ripley prepares – and she demonstrates her new earnestness by tying her wild hair up behind her head – she is stopped by the plaintive, faraway cry of Jones, the cat. Now, I am likely a little fonder of cats than the next man, but I'm bound to say that this Jones has gone beyond the limits of what any cat should get away with.

By now, Parker and Lambert are in the dank, austere and ill-lit parts of the *Nostromo*, near the heavy machinery, collecting cylinders of coolant – a noisy business – which they gather on a trolley. Parker is stalwart still, but Lambert is a nervous wreck.

Back in the soft white light and the lustrous silence of the shuttle, Ripley finds Jones's cage and goes hunting him. She moves about, stealthily, but not as secretly as the camera which effortlessly conveys the chance of aliens waiting to pounce on her. She finds Jones: there is another great scare as the cat jumps out from a hiding place. Ripley is scratched. But she retrieves the marmalade cat and puts him in his cage.

Lambert is at work, but then a dangling shadow obtrudes on her image. It is the alien (maybe coolant is his candy). Parker sees it, too. Lambert is paralysed, and Parker is afraid of firing his flame-thrower for fear of hitting her (a feeble excuse, agreed).

Ripley now hears them on the radio speaker system – she had not heard them before (it is another ploy one has to forgive). But she can tell the peril they are in.

The monster towers over Lambert. She cannot move.

Parker charges at it, from behind. The monster whirls round – a terrific, cutting change – and strikes at him. It holds his bloodied figure in the air. Then it turns and we see one tendril hooking round Lambert's ankle and reaching up her leg. Over the radio, Ripley hears screams of terror. Then there was one.

18

Ripley sees what must be a foot and a leg belonging to Lambert, hanging in the air, blood-stained. Parker is slumped over his own fatal wound. She is distraught – and, let it be said, this Ripley's face (though Sigourney Weaver was in her late twenties) can suggest the frightened little girl. And if *Alien* is Ripley's battle for respect (and even command), still in these parts of the film we feel the threat of immaturity and collapse. Also, once Ripley is alone, Weaver's performance becomes more naked and primitive – she can abandon Ripley's man-like reserve now, her self-control.

She runs headlong down the corridors in panic – there is a hand-held, first-person tracking shot. And, when she reaches the controls, she pulls all the switches that will explode the ship.

Sirens start a steady honking that goes on for the next several minutes. And then a voice like a telephone operator's voice – English – announces, 'The Emergency Destruct System is now active. The ship will destruct in T minus ten minutes.' The override control can only be activated in the first five minutes. (This voice is referred to in the credits as the Voice of 'Mother' – and it is played by Helen Horton.)

With the Destruct System activated, the lights are flashing, steam is emitted from the walls and the temperature seems to rise. (It might be thought that in this day and age – whenever it is – destruction is a simple matter that does not require all this stress. But at least the search for coolant is explained.)

Ripley picks up the cage and retreats towards the shuttle. The voice tells us that the override control elapses in T minus three minutes.

And then she sees the monster, waiting for her. In alarm, she puts down Jones's cage and manages to slide away to retreat. There is a shot of the dripping black steel jaws of the alien confronting the gingery, out-of-focus Jones. The voice says T minus one and it begins a countdown at thirty seconds as Ripley tries to avert the explosion. Why? To save Jones? Or because the heat is intolerable?

She fails to reverse everything before the voice gets to zero. She calls out to Mother to do something for the cooling system, but there is no response. For the first time, Ripley gets properly angry. She goes back in what is a splendid shot in half-light, advancing, crouched, carrying the flame-thrower, its muzzle breathing flame. This is one of the great shots of an action woman in the history of film.

The lights flash. The sirens throb. She sees Jones — this must be where she saw the monster, but it is gone for now. She picks up the cage and staggers at last into the shuttle area.

The voice says there is only one minute left to abandon the ship.

Ripley goes to the shuttle controls and starts to hit switches.

She straps herself in.

We see the shuttle lower itself from the body of the *Nostromo*.

The voice is at 30–29–28.

It takes off.

In an overhead window, she sees the underside of the ship passing above. Then it recedes.

10–9–8.

In the window, we see an intense, horizontal line of light as the ship explodes. Ripley is burnished and white in the blast. The shuttle rattles.

There is a second and a third explosion.

A rush of flame-coloured light comes towards the shuttle. Then it dies and shrinks back to nothing. The black of space resumes.

Ripley has got away.

19

But she cannot be alone. We knew that in 1979, and we did not mean Jones — though surely there might be a way in which the alien had co-opted or penetrated the cat. Didn't we see them last examining each other? Suppose that Ripley picked up Jonesy for a croon and cuddle and realised, 'What big teeth you have'?

No, it's not that. The film is most plainly not over yet. Which surely means that, somehow, the monster got into the shuttle. Ahead of Ripley. In other words, it not only divined her strategy, but had some way of recognising and tapping the entry system so that it could get into the shuttle and find a hiding-place. That presupposes not just a creature with deft, physical skills – call it touch – but a capacity for thinking ahead that is worthy of a scriptwriter. What force has driven this picture? Is it the Company, the crew, or the beast? Our best clue to answering that is the certainty that this escaped, relaxed Ripley – so youthful now – is not quite safe yet.

Like a little girl home alone, Ripley strips off and plays with the cat. She is getting ready for bed, for that big sleep to cover the months of space that remain. She takes off her overalls, letting them fall on the floor like a kid, until the tall, athletic Weaver is left in nothing but the skimpiest of briefs and a half T-shirt.

There were observations in 1979 that the movie's stirring tribute to a woman's courage and effectiveness still reduced the lead actress to the level of a voyeur's delight – and guys do remember this scene. Sigourney Weaver was nothing short of awesome, and her underwear was spotless white, no matter the trying time Ripley had had. Still, her disrobing subtly supports the menace of more to come: she is staked out for us, and for story – and so there grows an inescapable conclusion, that we and the monster are watching her together. Is there glue hanging from our lascivious gaze?

Ripley opens a sleeping bin – one of those padded coffins we saw at the start. She puts Jones in, and then goes around the shuttle adjusting controls. It is then that the last gotcha! of *Alien* occurs, as a hand, or a claw, drops down from the wall to meet hers. For those dark grey pipes we thought we saw are not just the wall of the shuttle – they are the monster folded up in wicked waiting. This is not a casual trick, I think; the alien is innately attuned to technological forms – that was surely evident in Giger's huge monster tomb on the deserted planet. Yet it is also a dynamic, organic creature, one that incorporates our entire sense of reptiles and prehistoric animals. Thus, in the ultimate nightmare, futuristic forms turn into primeval, visceral shapes.

Ripley becomes braver, yet more childlike, under threat. She stands up to the alien, out-thinks and defeats it. But she starts to sing to herself, fragments of childhood songs, like a kid who has battled fear of the dark. And, all the time, her resolve is very close to the panic of collapse. So her mind and her being have to steel themselves against the hideous, foul suggestiveness of the alien. It is reason versus atmosphere, at close quarters.

She goes into a kind of wardrobe closet where a spacesuit is hanging. It is there, waiting to be filled, and from a low angle we see the half-naked woman stepping into the suit. This is agile and nearly magical, but it is very sexual, too. We see her nipples as hard as switches under the T-shirt. We see her long legs manoeuvring. But she gets in and puts the helmet on. Why?

She has a plan. She gets a harpoon gun and loads it. And then she frees what seems like steam in the walls, forcing the alien out of its hiding-place. At that, she opens the hatch – the void is gaping and sucking at the ship. The creature is spreadeagled in the doorway. Ripley shoots it with the harpoon. It falls back – this figure is plainly a human being in a suit. The hatch closes and the alien bounces against the side of the shuttle briefly before it is gone.

And now peace floods in. Ripley will sleep, but she records her final memo to the log – how she alone has survived, a kind of Ishmael.

After that, we see her sleeping face beneath the plastic lid of the coffin. Are only those asleep safe? Or are all schemes of safety flawed?

The end.

Interlude

The poster for *Alien* had one of the alien eggs, in darkness, but igniting at its lower end. The ad line was 'In space no one can hear you scream.' The film was rated 'R' in the United States and preview screenings had given ample evidence that audiences would be upset. Some of the Fox executives were alarmed that they might get blamed for so 'disturbing' a picture. (As David Giler put it, '*Alien* is to *Star Wars* what the Rolling Stones are to the Beatles; it's a *nasty Star Wars*.') Today, it is hard to imagine executives entertaining such reservations.

The film did very well: by the end of 1979, Fox reported rentals from all over the world of $48.4 million. As such, it was the fourth biggest grosser of the year, coming after *Rocky II*, *Every Which Way But Loose* and *Superman*. (Incidentally, *Star Wars*, in its first re-release, took in another $11 million.) Some people reckoned that *Alien* could have done even better, for it was given a slow platform release – it opened in only 91 theatres, followed by a broad national release a few weeks later. Yet granted the heavy TV advertising, and the shock effect it possessed, surely it could have exploited a bigger immediate spread. Some experts believed it was maybe $10 million down because of that decision – enough to have put it in second place for the year.

The movie was nominated for two Oscars – for art direction, and for visual effects. (Best Picture that year went to *Kramer vs. Kramer*, with *Norma Rae* and *Apocalypse Now* as other contenders – the latter the big 'Conrad' movie of that year.) In the first category, it lost to *All That Jazz*, but in the second it won. H. R. Giger, Carlo Rambaldi,

Brian Johnson, Nick Allder and Denys Ayling all received statuettes
(from Farah Fawcett). It's worth stressing that so many of these visual
effects were real and designed. They were Giger's art, transformed by
film, and not the electronic engineering that was to come. In that
sense, the *Alien* films do not cheat; they create their world for the
camera – and are thus a little old-fashioned.

Alien had a fairly good press. In *Sight and Sound*, Philip Strick called
it 'gorgeous, leisurely'. Despite the critical tendency to take the horror
action lightly, and to see such monsters as a sign of exploitation,
some people saw and felt how much Ridley Scott had done. They
responded to the claustrophobia of this unique haunted house, to
the strange rapport between the *Derelict* and the aliens, to the funky
crew, and to Sigourney Weaver. Making her the survivor paid off
handsomely, and though her character was only faintly delineated, the
actress received large amounts of mail which showed how far Ripley
had impressed strangers: 'Most of the letters I got were sincere and
sweet and I appreciated the compliments and sentiments. But I had
trouble with the ones that said, "You must write me today. I can't live
unless you write me now! You are the *only* person who can understand
what I'm feeling." What can you write back to these people?' Weaver
was sent gifts and flowers. Her agent had never known anything like
it. Was this just because Weaver seemed attractive and appealing? Or
was Ripley a security figure in a very dangerous world?

Let's follow the money for the moment. The box-office splash that
early summer was enough to have Fox executives talking gleefully of a
sequel. However, by the end of the year *Alien* was still, technically, in
the red. The would-be profit participants – Brandywine, O'Bannon
and Shusett, notably – were dismayed to see an end-of-year statement
that reported, so far, a net loss on the movie of $2.4 million.

How did that compute? Domestic rentals were $37 million; $3.9
million had come in from Britain and Europe; and $7 million from
the rest of the world. But the expenses looked like this:

distribution fee	$15.4 million
advertising costs	$15.7 million
prints, etc.	$3.1 million
taxes, etc.	$914,000
checking and collection	$235,000
trade fees	$229,000
foreign versions	$312,000
shipping	$168,000
miscellaneous	$227,000
interest on negative cost	$1.7 million
over budget	$1.9 million
negative cost	$10.79 million

The *Alien* numbers received a lot of attention in the general press, for this seemed like a glaring example of what many people in pictures complained of as 'creative accounting' so as to ensure that the profit participants (the producer, the director, the writer and the actors) rarely saw back-end money on even famously successful films. But notice the structural conditions implicit in the figures above.

First of all, the distributor can charge every single item of marketing or promotion expense against a picture, and still pull in a distribution fee of just over 30 per cent in this case. It charges the cost of the movie, an alleged over-run (disputed in the case of *Alien*), and interest at 125 per cent of the prime rate. More or less those sorts of terms are standard. Moreover, no one on *Alien* had a contract that gave them participation points on the gross – as opposed to the net – income. Gross participants claim their percentage on every incoming dollar from the first one earned. Net participants only start to earn when a picture goes into profit.

In fact, profit on *Alien* began with the next statement: by July 1980, its rentals were $61.4 million – that actually showed a more robust ongoing business than was usual, and it meant profit of $4 million. It may also reflect some decision at Fox to tidy up the numbers, or be

more generous. For, plainly, there are several items under expenses
that are difficult to verify or track down. For example, 'checking
and collection' refers to the sometime need to push exhibitors for
a prompt accounting – let alone an accurate one. Also, the total for
prints suggested far more copies of *Alien* than anyone had ever seen
being used.

What are the lessons of all this? That it is always wise in pictures
to get your money *up front* and as a gross participant; that being in
distribution is not quite as ruinous as the distributors sometimes claim;
and that collaboration reaches its most painful stage long after a movie
has been finished. It also points to the special place of Brandywine
in the *Alien* pictures: after the Fox logo, all have been labelled a
'Brandywine Production'. That means that Gordon Carroll, Walter
Hill and David Giler so managed the making of the first picture
that they became the production entity. Brandywine made the film,
and has stood in line as a legal owner of the sequels. All absolutely
legitimate, and essential to the picture business – as well as some
compensation for the loss of the writing credit. O'Bannon never
reappeared. Plus, do not forget: the producers have the rare chance
in movie-making of testing their skills and their dreams with someone
else's money.

Disputes and suspicions aside, there was talk of a sequel. Ridley Scott
actually went on to make *Blade Runner*, a significant step forward in
adult science fiction, and a movie that further explored the difficulty
in telling replicants from human beings, as well as the pathos of the
life-like machine. *Blade Runner* was in many ways a child of *Alien*,
but it *was* set on Earth in an altered yet emotionally recognisable
L. A. When asked what a possible *Alien* sequel ought to be about,
Scott said, 'It should certainly explain what the alien is and where
it comes from. That will be tough because it will require dealing
with other planets, worlds, civilisations. Because obviously the alien
did come from some sort of civilisation . . . The alien may be one

Eighteen years - or several centuries - in Company service have their effect on Ellen Ripley and Sigourney Weaver. The young crew member waits to be delivered of her child - and all the two stages of woman have in common is that faraway look.

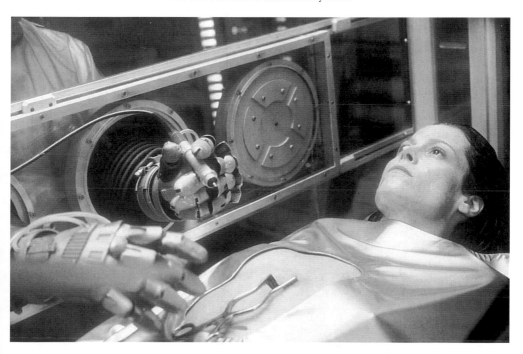

Explorations on the planet that discover the fantastic vision of H.R. Giger.

The Alien itself, in a rare, thoughtful moment.

Ripley battles with Ash; and Bishop makes ready to bring in a rescuing module.

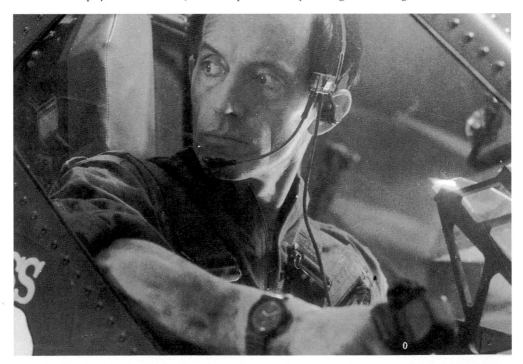

of the last descendants of some long-lost self-destructed group of beings.'

David Giler said, as early as 1979, that he and Walter Hill were working on a sequel, though he dismissed suggestions that Jones the cat had been planted at the end of *Alien* as the new host to the monster. But Scott made it clear that he had never felt the need for an intellectual explanation of the monster. He didn't need to know its origins in *Alien* or its 'meaning': 'It has absolutely no message. It works on a very visceral level and its only point is terror, and more terror.'

That said, the original *Alien* was a standing-up for the notion that one brave, resourceful woman might defeat the terror and that she could rise above the intrigue of a robot and a devious Company. There was also the clear awareness that knowledge was not necessarily worthwhile for its own sake: for if an alien existed in the universe, maybe it was best eliminated, rather than brought home for study. In that sense, Ripley is an old-fashioned soldier who would rather kill the enemy than risk understanding it. That so decent and morally unshakeable a young American woman laid claim to that duty was striking: at a profound level the film said, trust common sense, not technology, advanced knowledge, or the rarefied claims of science.

But something else is set up in that first film, something that, I suspect, no one intended, but which would hang over sequels. Sigourney Weaver was sometimes asked how she felt about the way Ripley stripped down to her underwear at the end of *Alien*. The actress never felt a hint of our voyeurism. Once upon a time, she said, there had been notions of a good deal of casual nudity in the film – a crew too slack to wear uniforms. Weaver added that, for her, the ending was something that made her think about the alien:

> You're almost seeing me through the alien's eyes. Suddenly I
> go from a dark green animal to a pink and white animal. Ridley
> and I had so much fun working out the ending. There were so

many different endings. One of them was that the alien would
surprise me and I would run into the closet where I'd take off
my suit and put on another. So there would have been a moment
when the alien would see me between suits and be fascinated.
Because the alien isn't evil. It's just following its natural instincts
to reproduce through whatever living things are around it.

Arguably, no one else had such sympathy for the monster – or felt as
open to it. It would be years before that insight came to fruition; but
even then, one thing was, if not established, then beginning to emerge
– that in any continuation of the story the relationship between the
alien and Ripley had to be persisted with. For it was something deeper
than antagonism.

A sequel did not leap into being. Fox had *The Empire Strikes Back*
and *Return of the Jedi* to concentrate on. *Blade Runner* shifted the tone
of science fiction back towards the darker end of the spectrum. Then
in 1984, a young writer-director out of the Roger Corman training
school, James Cameron, was given his chance at a real picture – *The
Terminator*, a relentless action movie that had a superb mythic parable
for a story, and which again featured the combative interaction of real
people and androids.

Aware of how much Scott had meant to the first *Alien* (but
unable to get him), and finding that their own Walter Hill could
still not be tempted into the genre, Brandywine saw Cameron as a
worthy inheritor of the *Alien* story-line. Hill and Giler sold him on
a treatment. Hill, Giler and Carroll would all get credit as executive
producers. But for the one and only time in the *Alien* quartet, a single
person – Cameron – would do the script and direct the film. He
further established his own control when he enlisted his wife, Gale
Anne Hurd, to serve as producer. Cameron, who came from Canada,
was only thirty-two. None too articulate in person, he had a driven
inner nature that welcomed conflict with authority figures and would
often challenge and tease the 'veteran', Sigourney Weaver. Already,

Cameron was the kind of man happy to stake his vision against great odds (and the doubts of others) – as such, he was preparing for *Titanic*, whether he knew it or not.

Once again, it was arranged for the shooting to be done in England – at Pinewood this time. But although Giger was credited again for his original *Alien* designs, the effects on *Aliens* were created by Stan Winston (who had done *The Terminator*), with assistance from the L.A. Effects Group. Robert and Dennis Skotak were hired to supervise the other visual effects. Adrian Biddle did the photography. Ray Lovejoy was editor (he had edited *2001* and *The Shining*), and James Horner did the music (he had done *Star Trek II*, *48 Hours* and *Cocoon*). Virtually the entire production team, therefore, was changed. Beyond the studio system and seven-year contracts, crews rarely stay together. So story continuity is all the harder to protect – and all the more reliant on its inner strength.

But Sigourney Weaver was Ripley again, for at least $2 million this time, a big increase for her yet not an exceptional fee for a lead actor (her career had built with *The Year of Living Dangerously* and *Ghostbusters*, in both of which she was clearly a secondary figure). In addition, Cameron brought in several supporting players from *The Terminator* – Michael Biehn, Lance Henriksen and Bill Paxton. The second picture in the series had taken a long time to come and it cost over $20 million, but it was the most trouble-free of all the productions, just as it would prove the most exhilarating of the films.

Weaver appreciated Cameron's enlargement of Ripley – and they got on well. But there was an intriguing area of disagreement. Cameron was obsessed with survival, and destroying the creatures. But the actress saw something more in the alien, a species with its own needs. 'I was the throttle,' said Cameron, 'and she was the brakes.'

ALIENS

1

There is that sound of wind, sighing or mere presence, set off by the bass notes of music, that stands so well for the unimaginable depth of space. Blue lattice forms appear in the centre of the screen, and as the first credits pass by, so those lines become the letters of *ALIENS* – so simple a change of title, so geometric a progression. Then the 'I' in the word goes from its royal blue to an intense, scalding white that floods the whole screen, bursts, and gives way to the blue and black strands of space.

The camera tilts gently down across this panorama, and so we see, in the centre of the image, a tiny six-sided figure, grey but shadowed, approaching us. A pellet, a bullet? It is a shuttle – let us say it is the shuttle from *Alien*, the observation windows eyes in the head- or helmet-like shape. It comes rapidly, towards us, and then passes beneath us – just as if it knew where it was going.

Inside the shuttle, there is a gloom faintly illuminated by the glow from outside. We see coils, pipes and tubing in the walls of the craft, enough to remind us of the monster's last hiding-place. But only the camera moves now. As it passes across the shuttle we see a crystalline dew on the surface of a chair. There is the same rime of time and condensation on all the surfaces. Yet as we come to the plastic-covered coffins, the sleeping compartment, we can see enough through the lid to know that Ripley is there, asleep, lying on her back, at peace, hardly aged, a Sleeping Beauty still.

Then a beam of light slides over the lid. A computer screen rattles into life with the message 'PROXIMITY ALERT'.

From outside, you see the shuttle drawn or sucked into the maw of a far larger, circular ship – more a city than a vessel. We hear the

heavy clunk of docking, done without any effort from the shuttle –
it could be commanded by some inescapable magnetic force.

Then, from inside the shuttle, we hear and see something like a laser
burning through the door – or the wall that included the doorway. In
short order, this bright light – white, and orange where the burning
occurs – cuts out a shape, and the door falls inwards.

In the light of the opening, a crane, a mobile tool, peers in. It has
a narrow, blue scanning light that is drawn across the interior. This
machine has a mantis-like form – it could be some evolved version
of the aliens we remember. But after it has made its examination, it
withdraws. Two human figures then enter: they wear spacesuits and
gas masks. We can hear them breathing.

The gloved hand of one of these figures wipes the frost off the lid of
the coffin. We see Ripley more clearly, asleep still, and as the camera
pans down, we can make out the legs, the paws, and even the head,
of Jones, the marmalade cat, still asleep. One of the figures takes off
its helmet. A voice reports that Ripley is alive.

'There goes our salvage,' says another.

2

The camera, from space, pans across a distant view of a planet on
which we can make out some familiar land-masses from Earth. Then
it comes to an elaborate space station – a framework with several
block-like structures that have illuminated windows – that seems to
be in Earth orbit.

We cut to a hospital room, presumably inside this structure. A nurse
moves in front of a window that shows us part of the space station.
'How are we, then?' she asks. Ripley struggles to sit up and says she
feels awful. Better than yesterday, the nurse tells her, and then, 'Looks
like you've got a visitor.'

The doors to the room slide open, and a man (Paul Reiser) comes
in, carrying Jones. This man is in his early thirties. He wears a grey

suit exactly from the 1980s, except that its little collar is turned up; he has nearly a pompadour of dark, curly hair. He wears a red tie.

Ripley seems better as soon as she sees Jones. 'Come 'ere,' she says, sitting up to make a lap for the cat. She wears a white hospital gown. The man sits down the wrong way round on a chair and introduces himself as Carter Burke, a Company man – but 'I'm really an OK guy,' he tries to reassure her. It is in the external indicators of Paul Reiser – and the decision to cast him – that this cheeriness casts its own cold shadow. Reiser is not warm, not easily trusted, (not even after years of *Mad About You*, on TV, with the reassuring company of Helen Hunt).

Ripley cannot help but be wary. She gazes at him, and seems to see the shiftiness. 'How long was I asleep?' she asks.

Burke affects to be taken aback by this. He asks her whether this matter hasn't been discussed with her yet. She says no, and he has to admit that her 'hyper-sleep' (he's vague about the exact condition) lasted fifty-seven years. Ripley smiles and starts to laugh. But then the possibility overtakes her.

Burke prattles on about how she had drifted through the core system until a deep salvage team found her – a thousand-to-one chance. 'You're damned lucky to be alive, kiddo. You could be floating out there for ever.' Like the last monster she expelled from the shuttle. Like the swathed corpse of Kane.

The realisation sends Ripley into a reverie in which she starts to moan and feel pain in her body.

Jones turns and hisses at some intrusive being within her.

Ripley cries out. The cat runs away. She writhes and arches her back. We see a close-up of Jones's pink tongue and his teeth. Ripley knocks away the things on her bedside table. Burke calls for help. She cries out to God and tells the frantic staff, 'Kill me!' Then she pulls up her white gown, and there, between the navel and her ribs, we see an imminent eruption, a blunt head, like a periscope coming up out of the sea.

She wakes. It was a dream, wasn't it?

3

By any movie standards, it is a dream, from which Ripley reawakens, clutching a knot in her stomach where the alien was about to appear. And it is very important that, already, she has imagined herself as some kind of interfered-with, invaded mother, just as the dream was there to reassure old loyalists that this was *Alien* still (for the terrible delivery that Kane submits to remained the touchstone shock of the first film). But if the scene *is* a dream, what are we to make of the information it contains? After all, Burke will be a character in the rest of *Aliens*. He is real; the hospital is the place where Ripley is recovering. Was she really on her way back fifty-seven years? This is not just a question that hinges on how her shuttle got lost, and whether space is enormous enough to contain fifty-seven years of drift; obviously it is, but so what? What is more telling is that, if these aliens mean to conquer the world, why are they so patient? Have they been content just to be monstrous by themselves on their desolate planet that long? Would you?

And if the Company has been behind so much – as witness Burke's prompt, creepy solicitude – why did they let Ripley 'drift' so long? Weren't they, somehow, monitoring the shuttle? Aren't they 'the Company'? It's a strange riddle, not really worked out by the film, but it doesn't take away from the shock of fifty-seven years – even if nothing much seems to have happened to Ripley in that time except for her hair getting shorter. But what does happen in hyper-sleep? The films are too busy to say. That's understandable, yet a missed chance, too: for surely hyper-sleep must mean the beginning of a loss of context or humanity? After all, if Ripley has been away fifty-seven years, then wouldn't we expect her parents to be dead? If people in this time still have parents in the same old way. Surely they do; otherwise, Ripley's dread of raped parenthood – kill me! she asks; she has no doubts – wouldn't be what it is.

4

When Ripley wakes from her bad dream, the voice of the nurse – the nurse from the dream – asks, 'Bad dreams again?' She offers Ripley something to make her sleep, but Ripley reckons she has slept enough. What solace is sleep if it frees such dreams? Apart from the induced and maybe frozen hiatuses that span great distances, there is not much human sleep in these pictures. Is there a tablet that serves instead?

She picks up the cat and cuddles it. It might be supposed that no sick room would let an animal remain on a patient's bed. But, recollect, Jones was only brought there in her dream – by the suspicious Burke. Yet now she holds the cat and croons to it, her only friend in the world, no matter that its fierce jaws were so close to monstrousness. There is an ambiguity in caring, or motherhood; and Ripley cannot escape it.

Then we cut to a smoke-filled conference room, illuminated by angular strip lighting. There is a screen that carries pictures of the *Nostromo* crew and their resumés. Ripley is standing, turning, moving, impatient, and all the people around the conference table are still. Many of them are smoking. How has our future gone astray? A Dr Van Leuwen heads the inquiry. He wears the same high-collared suit jacket we saw on Burke – and Burke is there, too.

The inquiry observes that the *Nostromo* was detonated and destroyed – at her doing, Ripley insists. That's a cost of $42 million in modern dollars, someone observes, minus the payload. Technicians have examined the shuttle on which Ripley returned and found no trace of the creature she described. 'Good!' she bursts out. Someone asks if such a creature is found on LV426 (the official name of the planet on which the *Nostromo* landed). None, says a woman expert at the table; she is plain, sexless, and wears a tie.

Ripley's impatience cracks. 'Did IQs just drop while I was away?'

she wants to know. And it's an interesting question, for in all the *Alien* films there is a sense that as technology becomes more advanced, so 'intelligence' or 'common sense' has declined. Look, says Ripley, the creature wasn't indigenous to LV426 – it had come from elsewhere on a crashed ship. In over three hundred surveyed worlds, someone says, no creature like this has ever been noted.

'Thank you, Officer Ripley, that will be all,' says Dr Van Leuwen, drawing the inquiry to a close. But Ripley explodes. 'God damn it!' she cries – and her nightmare dismay falls away – 'That's not all!' Burke winces at her manners, and she reminds them all of the eggs on LV426, waiting.

She picks up the papers of official reports and dismisses them as 'bullshit'. Burke sighs. We see a computer screen which notes that the file is closed.

The meeting breaks up. Burke comes up to Ripley and tells her, 'That could have been better.' But Ripley only wants to get at Van Leuwen. At least check the planet out, she asks. The doctor smiles in a superior way: 'I don't have to.' For it turns out that people have been living on LV426 for twenty years or so – terra-formers, they are called, making the air breathable on the planet. It's what is called a shake-and-bake planet, he tells her. How many people? she asks, in dread. Sixty or seventy families, he surmises. Families.

5

In close-up, smoke is drifting upwards. The camera tilts down and we see Ripley's hand hanging down. It is a suggestive (even foreboding) image, moving across the back of her hand to the fingers, and then to find the cigarette itself, held in her fingertips, its long edge of ash smouldering. We think less of Ash, straightaway, than the way in which her fine, long hand – it is Weaver's hand – resembles those Giger shapes we saw on the surface of LV426. It is a lovely hand – if you like – but it is in some sort of limb-like league with claws we have seen. The basic forms of life so easily slip over from one species to another.

The camera moves to Ripley's sad profile, gazing at the cigarette and her own hand, and thinking what? A long shot places her in her grey room, alone except for Jones.

Then, in the corridor outside, we see Burke and Lieutenant Gorman (William Hope), wearing uniform and a peaked cap. They stop at Ripley's door and press the buzzer. She opens the door, but closes it again as soon as she realises who's there. She doesn't believe in any mercy for her solitude.

Burke always becomes more nervous when he's rebuffed or challenged: he uses fluttering hand movements, widened eyes and a querulous tone – the stock in trade of Paul Reiser. He admits now, speaking to the closed door, that something has come up. The Company has lost contact with LV426. There is a close-up of Ripley's face in the reopened doorway. She is confirmed, in a way; yet more vulnerable, too.

A small time-cut follows, and we are inside her room. She is making coffee for the two men, and already rejecting Burke's suggestion that she go back. He tries to persuade her that Gorman and the Colonial Marines can handle anything. They have state-of-the-art firepower. Gorman agrees, though he seems less confident than Burke.

She says she has to go to work. Oh, sure, says Burke, pouncing – in the cargo dock, isn't it? She agrees. It's all she can get, working with loaders and forklifts. Burke knows all of this; maybe he has arranged the humiliation. Then he tells her he could get her back as Flight Officer: the Company will pick up her contract – if she goes. 'It's a second chance, kiddo,' he says in cold palliness. 'You need to face this thing.'

She cuts him off. She's already had her 'psych evaluation'. But he jumps her again. He's seen it. He knows she wakes up every night in a sweat.

I'm not going back, she tells him.

He lowers his head; his hand goes to his mouth. He is a little boy, told off. OK, he says, but he leaves her his phone card, in case she has second thoughts.

6

Something remarkable is happening – let us not miss it in the busy set-up of a new story; let us realise, instead, how far the old story is recurring. LV426 is apparently a run-of-the-mill place, and yet the decision has been taken to set up a shake-and-bake colony there. What that means, as far as we can judge, is the building of an enormous plant – powered by . . . ? – to make the atmosphere on the planet breathable. Suppose, for the sake of argument, that it is a small planet, one where a man could hardly take an afternoon stroll without going over the early curve of the horizon. Still, imagine the expense of making that once harsh atmosphere human-friendly – and marvel that this same society would even notice $42 million on a lost cargo ship.

But why has LV426 been made inhabitable? No one even bothers to mention mineral wealth there, let alone rare pleasures of climate or view. Whenever we see it, it seems a wretched, unusable place. But, without air, it could hardly be the site of the exuberant battle planned for *Aliens*. Even so, when so much is done that is flagrantly implausible, we forgive it or even miss it if it is for a character's destiny. Strong presence is more factual in a movie than arguments of cause and effect.

Then consider one thing more. When last we saw LV426 it was a very pregnant place, loaded with eggs waiting to hatch. We saw one let its young out into the world – the one that grew so fast Ripley was hard-pressed to hurl it into space. And fifty-seven years now have passed, during which something like two hundred terra-former colonists settled on LV426, made their home there, yet never noticed or were disturbed by the eggs and their offspring? Whereas, now, within days of Ripley being returned to civilisation, or a waking state, the signal from LV426 cuts out.

It can mean only one thing. That the alien intelligence has been waiting for Ripley, and that somehow they know she is ready again. They want *her* – the story begins to resemble a tale of irrational desire or yearning. But there is an extra implication: that the aliens are so close to the source of the story that they are its drivers or its tellers.

Question: do they want vengeance, or Ripley? Do they just want her for her own sake? Further, would you go back if you were Ripley, knowing what she knows, or would it take some unfathomable, absurd but irresistible desire to carry you back? We are at a place where the most imperative longings are exactly congruent with the impulse and ritual of story. Something has chosen Ripley for the ultimate ordeal.

7

We see Ripley alone in her room again, pondering her position. Then, on a cut, it is the middle of the night and she jerks up into full close-up, woken from another troubled sleep. There is sweat on her, as well as the intricate pattern of lattice or blinds that masks a low-level night-light. By sitting up, and coming into the frame, she seems to face something that awaits her. But it is quite clear now, early in the second film – as it was not in the first – that Ripley is the focus of the film. Her close-ups take her importance for granted: she is being studied – but by whom or what?

She feels her chest, as if that old nightmare had been working. She wears a grey singlet. She weeps for a moment, and then goes to the wash-basin, runs water and rinses her face. The basin is very small, like one in a railway sleeper compartment. She examines herself in the mirror. It is not a young face any more, and not a happy one.

Without any more ado, she puts Burke's phone card into the telephone machine. It rings several times, and then Burke – naked, it seems − appears on the screen. 'Ripley,' he says − he can see her, too. 'You OK?'

She has only one question to ask him, that he's going back to LV426 to destroy the thing, not to study it.

'You have my word on that,' he answers.

But she keeps her eyes closed, and when she says, 'All right, I'm in,' it is not as if she is saying OK, fair enough, to get the monkey off my back I'll go back and do my bit. No, it's more that she tells herself, OK, they are lying, because all Burke does is lie, so it's the same shit, but I have no choice, I have to go back.

In which case, how does she know there is no choice? Has she felt the aliens' strange interest in her and recognised that nothing else in her life matches it?

She turns to Jones and tells him, little shithead, that he's staying here. There is a shot of the cat's inscrutable face that only reminds us of the inward confidence of all animal life next to these jittery people.

Then we see a ship moving grandly through space from left to right. This ship seems warlike; it bristles with turrets and guns, and the music is militaristic. Inside the ship, we pan across empty interiors to find a row of coffins − at least a dozen of them. There are also small puffs of steam as the ship functions. Just before the lids raise, and the lights come on, we see a list of names flicker up on the computer screen: GORMAN, APONE, HICKS, FERRO, VASQUEZ, DRAKE, SPUNKMAYER, DIETRICH, FROST, WIERZOWSKI, CROWE − and so on. There are other names, but the dissolving image slips away before we can note them. It will turn out that there may be as many as twenty people on the ship − the Colonial Marine contingent, plus Ripley and Burke.

A few of them wake and we see Ripley in her grey singlet and underpants. The movie sinks into that odd genre for a few minutes best expressed by Sergeant Apone − 'Another glorious day in the Corps.' He is the trusty, disciplinarian sergeant, hardcore: the first thing he did on waking was thrust the stub of an old cigar in his mouth. He rallies and rags on the Marines. We hear their small talk. We meet Drake, a raw-faced crewcut man, Hicks (Michael Biehn), a joker named Hudson (Bill Paxton), and Vasquez (Jenette Goldstein), a sultry, muscled Latina who is doing body-building exercises within a few minutes of waking.

'Hey, Vasquez,' asks the joker, 'have you ever been mistaken for a man?'

'No,' growls Vasquez, 'have you?'

And Drake gives her a handshake, grinning in delight, and tells her she's bad. No matter how far in the future we go, it seems, Marines are Marines.

Ripley is very much an outsider. 'She saw an alien once,' whispers Vasquez in a bitchy way, and the joker replies, 'Whoopee-fucking-do.' In all their hard pink and brown skins, they look like appetizers for our monster, shrimp waiting for dip, but, even if we know enough to be amused by their bravado, there is an air of true comradeship that is central to *Aliens*. It's a movie made with nostalgia for organisations like the Corps – its sour repartee, its order and sacrifice, and its hardware (all of which, I suspect, are felt by Canada's James Cameron).

We cut forward to find most of the contingent in the mess hall, having their first meal. There is a communal table, but the 'grunts' mutter to the effect that 'the new lieutenant' doesn't eat with them. He's at the top of the table with Burke and Ripley. There are the old jokes about cornbread – service diet hasn't changed – and some macho remarks about colonists' daughters and their virginity. Ripley is not impressed.

One man a little older than the others, and a good deal more gaunt, stands near the table. He wears dark blue coveralls. His name is Bishop (Lance Henriksen), and, rather against his will, he is collared by some of the guys to do his routine with them. Someone holds Hudson's hand flat on the table, the fingers spread apart. Bishop holds a knife – not a piece of cutlery but a classic Bowie knife – with which he does a dance in and out of the spaces between Hudson's fingers. This trick begins fast, but then becomes supernatural in speed. The joker gazes down at his own avoided hand, screaming quietly in woe and amazement. Most of the others make an audience for the display. And when it is done, Bishop thanks Hudson – as if some relief has been given him.

Bishop then moves to the head of the table, carrying a dish of cornbread, which he offers to Gorman and Burke. As he sits down, he notices that in the work with the knife he has nicked himself – but he bleeds that thin white ooze we saw in Ash. Ripley, sitting next to him, sees this and recoils. No one told her there was an android on board.

Burke is taken aback: every ship has a synthetic, he says.

And the wide-eyed Bishop gently asks for the term 'artificial person' instead – he seems to be 'sensitive'.

'Is this a problem?' he wonders, and Burke remembers Ripley's Ash experience. He outlines it briefly. 'I'm shocked,' says Bishop. Was it an old model?

Burke agrees that Ash must have been a Hyperdyne 128–2.

Ah well, says Bishop, the 28–2s always were a bit 'twitchy'. As for himself, he boasts quietly, in the language of guarantee, it's impossible for him to harm, or 'allow to be harmed', a human being.

Ripley is unmoved. She knocks his food tray aside and tells Bishop to keep out of her way.

8

Lance Henriksen is the new model – not just less twitchy than Ian Holm, but more serene and idealistic, more overtly gay next to Ash's closeted or smothered nature. From New York, Henriksen had been seen a good deal in the 'seventies and early 'eighties. He had played Wally Schirra in Phil Kaufman's *The Right Stuff*, and this author met him at that time and noted his unusual edge – ambitious, yet ironic. He had been in James Cameron's *The Terminator*, too, but it was as

Bishop, here, that he made his most profound and influential impact. For Bishop is a role as good as that of Ash; and Bishop goes on, just as Henriksen's career would turn into *Near Dark* and the TV series *Millennium*. Let us just say for now that Henriksen has one of the great, arresting faces of our time, as well as a manner that leads us directly into the mysteries of personality and the question what is artificial? He is one of a type of actor who *could* be robots, and who have seen some limits to 'human authenticity'. For realise, we are in an age when computer-generated imagery can clone the stars of the past, and cast James Dean with Marilyn Monroe.

9

In some cargo hold on this ship, Lieutenant Gorman gathers the crew together for a briefing. They had left 'Gateway' too suddenly for an earlier delivery of information. But Gorman reveals his own greenness: he confuses Hudson and Hicks. And he cannot chill Hudson out of the insolent question, 'Is this going to be a stand-up fight, or a bug hunt?' (Does that mean that sometimes the Corps have battles, or wars, with other humans – while knowing what it is to be sent after 'bugs'? What other aliens might there be in three hundred known worlds – and what should we call them?)

Gorman calls upon Ripley to explain what happened on LV426. She does a fair job of it, and Hicks and Hudson both seem impressed. But Vasquez is impatient. She makes the shape of a gun with her hands and promises, 'I only need to know *one* thing – where they are.'

There is more verbal by-play, all of which suggests Gorman's lack of control. But Ripley makes clear the damage her alien can do. Gorman tells the crew that her full report is available for study on disk. Hudson asks how he might get out of this chicken-shit outfit, and the vexed Gorman dumps a whole lot of preparatory work on the crew in the next eight hours.

We see the ship progressing in the indigo night of space, but now it is like a crab that intrudes on the circle of LV426 – which seems a substantial planet.

Aboard the ship, the crew are busy at work in the equipment dock, loading missiles. Ripley appears and goes up to Apone and Hicks. She tells them she feels like a fifth wheel, and says she'd like to help. What can you do? asks Apone – there is something here of sexual interest as well as the manly challenge. Ripley nods at an elaborate, heavy loader – a metal suit in which the worker inserts himself. I can drive that, she says. Be my guest, says Apone.

Then he and Hicks watch, with mounting respect, as she enters the machine, turns it on, and sets to work. Indeed, she uses the claws to pick up two heavy blocks, then pauses, looks at the two guys with a cocky grin and says, 'Where you want it?' They laugh generously – 'Bay 12, please,' says Apone, and we know that Ripley has made herself one of the gang, as well as someone who interests Hicks.

10

We come forward to find the Marines in the last stages of arms preparation. Magazines are slammed into breeches in that percussion movies have taught us. Vasquez does a sinister, slow dance with her huge weapon; and when we see Drake, making the same moves, we appreciate a kind of tango between them.

The shuttle craft that will ferry the Marines down to LV426 is warming up. Next we see the low-slung but massively blocked armoured personnel carrier in which the landing party will ride. We see individual Marines strapping on protective leggings – an odd mixture of futuristic equipment and ancient personal armour.

Apone's roar drives them on in that pastiche of Marine movies which may have become orthodoxy in the Corps. 'Move it, move it, move it – Absolute badasses!' They take their places in the personnel carrier, strapping themselves in for the flight. Gorman is at the control panel inside the APC, but it is Bishop who drives the vehicle up the ramp and into the shuttle.

'Ready,' shouts Hudson, 'ready to get it on!'

Flaps in the spaceship open. We see that Ferro is piloting the shuttle: she wears a helmet, Ray-Ban dark glasses and carmine lip gloss. The shuttle is lowered, prior to being released. We notice that Hicks is watching Ripley, though she is unaware of the attention.

That running-at-the-mouth commentary on his own nervous elation, Hudson, shouts out: 'Express elevator to hell – going down!' And the shuttle plunges downwards until Ferro regains power and leverage and answers in her sunny way – like we're going to the beach today, kids – 'We're in the pipes, five by five', the lovely, impenetrable jargon of space travel.

The craft encounters turbulence and, to make talk, Ripley asks Gorman how many landings he's made. Thirty-eight, he says, tensely, all simulated. How many combat? asks Vasquez. Two, he replies, including this one. And the hardened Marines exchange weary glances, a circle that now includes Ripley and Burke. Hicks has fallen asleep, the perfect Gary Cooper-like figure. Or is he a nod to Ray Hicks (Nick Nolte) in *Who'll Stop the Rain*?

The surface of LV426 appears in the windows. Ferro's smug voice says she's coming around for a 709-er. Now they can see the vast outline of the Atmosphere Processor – a gloomy suburb of a place. Burke tells Ripley it's all automatic. The Company made it. They fly on over the colonists' complex. Ripley observes no structural damage and some lights on still. But there is a mournful mood to those views, enhanced by the music, and there is some suggestion of the terribly simple life led there by colonists. It resembles a prison camp more than a career.

Then Gorman orders a landing, with the shuttle to make an 'immediate dust-off', then stay on station. The shuttle lands on its flat feet, and the APC drives out on to the surface of the unwelcoming planet. It is night, and it is raining.

11

The movie revels in the way these Marines advance on and enter the colonists' complex. The way one team covers another. And then the idea of Vasquez, carrying her gun as if it were a pine tree, a flashlight on the side of her head, a red bandanna tidying up her dark hair. That may remind us of Parker from *Alien*. But these Marines – despite their gimmicky firepower,★ are throwbacks to another age and another movie. They advance as they might have done under Sergeant Ryker (John Wayne) at Iwo Jima. But is that credible? This far in the future, facing a possible enemy along the lines Ripley has described, is it Corps strategy to send in human teams as exposed as this? Vasquez doesn't even wear a helmet. Or would there not be some robotic penetration unit designed to seek out danger? (There's an added mark of nostalgia in these soldiers – they wear a stars-and-stripes insignia.)

The compound is melancholy in its abandonment. Doors flap, and there is even a red 'BAR' sign glowing in the noir-ish mist. But these guys make an electrical by-pass that opens the sealed doors and so – in two teams, under Apone and Hicks – they enter the corridors. Gorman, Burke and Ripley watch from the APC, tracking the personal TV cameras that every soldier carries.

There is damage in the corridors, and rain falling in some places. But the strip lighting is on still, and though there are signs of small arms fire, and even a few explosions, there is not a body to be seen. The motion detector scanners show nothing. But in an office, there are half-filled coffee cups and a doughnut, half-eaten. Watching on the monitors, Ripley sees something on Hick's camera. She gets him to back up and they find a ragged hole in the floor. 'It looks melted,' Hicks reports, and Burke murmurs, 'Acid for blood.'

★As in *The Terminator*, Cameron developed guns that are essentially like weapons known in the 1980s, yet swollen and encrusted with boyish dreams. These are the guns boys draw for their imagined heroes – explosive and fetishistic.

Apone reports that the place is dead. Gorman decides that the area is secure. Ripley argues, but the lieutenant insists, and tells the soldiers that he's coming in. 'It's safe,' mocks Hudson. Inside, Apone tells Gorman of signs that the colonists had tried to seal one section, and erect barricades. But the defences failed.

They move into the operations control area of the complex and find several glass cylinders that hold small alien creatures. They seem to be dead until the wide-eyed Burke stares too close and a limb lashes out at him. Bishop says that most are dead. He reads notes near the cylinders that report how one creature was surgically removed from a man who died during the procedure. And these aliens are the size of the creature that came on board the *Nostromo* with Kane.

But then one of the movement sensors – such as the crew of the *Nostromo* had – picks up a signal. The soldiers track it until a form jumps across their path. They shoot at it. But the figure hides. Ripley looks into the hiding-place and sees the grubby face of a little girl. She pursues this child all the way into her den, where she takes her into her arms and reassures her. She sees a family photograph of the child: Rebecca Jordan (Carrie Henn).

Gorman tries to interrogate the girl, but he gets nowhere and pronounces her 'brain-locked'. Ripley takes over and gives the child hot chocolate. She starts to clean her face and solemnly pronounces the discovery of a little girl, rather pretty, underneath it all. In the close-ups of this sequence, we notice the same imprint of lines on the upper lips of Ripley and Rebecca. There is a family resemblance. But when Ripley calls her 'Rebecca' the girl refuses that name. She is 'Newt'. Only her brother Jimmy called her Rebecca. And he, and her parents, are dead.*

---

*In the subsequent laser-disc release of the film – seventeen minutes longer than the original – we saw Newt and the terra-former community on LV426, prior to alien attack. But the Newt seen then was the same age as the Newt seen now – so much for time travel.

By now, we have every reason to suppose that the colonists are all dead, or past saving. The absence of bodies shows the totality of their defeat. Yet Newt has survived. Is that because she is small, nocturnal, resilient − like her name? Or is it rather that the aliens have let one person escape their patrol, one person who will inevitably arouse a sense of maternal protectiveness in Ripley? In other words, is Newt an S.O.S., or a warning? Is she truly a survivor, or bait in a special trap of the emotions designed for Ripley? Are we more likely to believe that these aliens − the ones who timed their insurrection on LV426 − are careless, or thorough?

12

In the colony laboratory, Bishop, that apparently obedient creature, has seemingly followed a mission. He is examining one of the dead aliens from the glass cylinders. He is in rapture over it, his wide eyes not just full, but consumed. 'Magnificent, isn't it?' he sighs to Gorman.

Meanwhile, Hudson has located the colonists, by tracking the identifications they were all implanted with. On an electronic read-out, he finds them all gathered in part of the processing station. It's impossible to be sure whether they are alive or not. Gorman orders the teams to find out. They all board the APC and drive over to the processing plant. They enter by the main doors, and then the Marines disembark.

But this interior is not man-made. Rather, it resembles the suggestive bodily shapes found in the wrecked craft or creature the *Nostromo* crew discovered. What's more, this place is as hot as it seemed to Kane and the others − 'hot as the tropics'.

At this point, as Ripley, Gorman and Burke observe from the APC, Ripley foresees the danger of firing weapons in that place − for the primary heat exchange could explode. Worse than that, says Burke, this planet is a fusion reactor − there could be a thermonuclear explosion. So Gorman gives the order to turn in magazines. Only flame units can be deployed. The Marines are horrified and unwilling – they stand for those troops in Vietnam, or wherever, who were not permitted to use all the firepower available to them.

But this dismay is forgotten as they come upon the colonists – human figures hanging from the ceiling, but cocooned or wrapped in hardened membrane. There is also an egg pod. A Marine reaches up to raise the head of one of these people, a woman, and her eyes open. 'Kill me!' she begs, and Ripley, watching from the APC, is jolted by the echo of her own dream. No sooner noted than the woman starts to cough or wretch. Her chest wall breaks open and the indignant, crimson snout of one of the alien infants appears, so demanding of life. A flame-thrower is used to incinerate the child and the mother.

This action has activated the aliens. Our view is not clear, in the dark, but we see the coils of enormous monsters rolling out of the walls like lazy boys struggling out of bed. Ripley tells Gorman to pull the Marines out. But a creature descends on one soldier so that his flame-thrower ignites, killing another – Crowe and Dietrich are gone in an instant. And now the aliens fall upon the Marines in the dark. A rattled Gorman calls to Apone to withdraw under cover of a suppressing fire from the incinerators. But Apone himself is seized from the rear by an alien. Gorman is in terror: 'Apone – talk to me?'

Ripley rages at Gorman to get the survivors out, but he is panic-locked and so Ripley takes control. Gorman fights back, but Burke takes her side. She drives the APC into the processing plant, and the Marines do what they can to retreat towards it. The APC charges through debris. The Marines kill some aliens. But the acid blood from one of them spills over a screaming Drake. Vasquez tries to save him and has to be dragged away.

The surviving Marines stagger into the APC, and as one alien jams itself in the doorway, so Hicks shoots it in the mouth with a shotgun. As Ripley drives away, an alien lands on the roof of the APC and lashes its way through the top hatch, trying to get at her. She brakes. The alien slides off the APC and falls on the ground. Whereupon, Ripley drives over it with the full force of the APC. She bursts through the doors of the plant and drives out on to the surface of the planet.

'Ease down,' Hicks tells her. She's broken a trans-axle.

We realise that those left are Ripley, Newt, Burke, Gorman (who has concussion), Vasquez, Hudson and Hicks. Everyone else is dead or gone in just a few moments of battle.

13

Vasquez counts the cartridges of nerve gas they have left: she reckons to shoot them into the processing centre. Ripley has a harder line. She proposes that they take off and just nuke the planet. Then Burke comes forward. He admits this is an emotional moment, but they can hardly conceive of the dollar value of the installation. 'They can bill me,' sneers Ripley. But Burke goes on. This is an important species, he says, you can't just destroy it. 'Watch me,' says Vasquez. 'I cannot authorise this,' says Burke.

Whereupon, Ripley makes her strategic play. 'I believe Corporal Hicks has authority here,' she says – the cross-stitching of close-ups between them has not been for nothing. And Hicks glances at her now, grateful yet not. Burke is flustered. How can a 'grunt' – no offence, he throws out; none taken, says Hicks – make that decision?

There's a pause, and then Hicks calls up Ferro on the radio, telling her to come in and get them. They'll nuke LV426. It's the only way to be sure, he says, and Ripley gives him the nicest face she's had in the whole movie. There's a feeling of fresh energy and purpose: the single imperative – destroy the aliens – is being heeded. There are enemies, in this philosophy, too total to be examined, even if their species is as magnificent as Bishop believes. Even if the species has already divined the conclusion that the shattered Marines would reach.

14

We see the survivors, carrying Gorman on a stretcher, making their way across the broken ground of LV426. Meanwhile on the ship, in orbit, Ferro gives orders to Spunkmayer to get under way. But as he enters the shuttle, he finds slime on the steps that lead to it. He says there's something wrong, but Ferro ignores him in her haste. We know what that slime indicates. But the more vexing question is how it got there. For when the shuttle let down on LV426, it was on the ground only long enough for the APC to disembark, and no more. We saw that – you can go back and look at it again – and in the few seconds the hatch was open nothing entered the shuttle. Or nothing we could see. But if an alien did get back to the ship on the shuttle, what else has it done? Either the scripting here is careless or desperate, or we are learning much more about the ultimate purposes of the creature.

All one can say for now is that the shuttle rescue fails. For as the shuttle comes in over the barren landscape, so Ferro calls to Spunkmayer, gets no response, turns round, and finds that a fully formed alien, jaws within jaws, with dire adhesions of slime, is her co-pilot. The creature strikes and blood soon covers the cockpit windows. The shuttle crashes and explodes. It is consumed in fire as those on the ground take shelter. Hudson begins to crack up, and Newt calmly supposes that they're not going home now. In which case, they'd better get back inside, she says, because the creatures mostly come at night.

Next, the survivors are in the operations centre, taking stock. They have pulse rifles, with fifty rounds each. There are fifteen M-40 grenades, and one flame-thrower. Ripley asks how long it will be before anyone thinks to send a rescue mission, and Hicks estimates seventeen days. Hudson is breaking down. But Ripley reminds him that Newt survived, without training or weapons – she passes over the question 'why?'. Instead, she gets Hudson to find a floor plan, to do something positive. The Marine rallies.

The floor plan establishes that it might be possible to isolate the medical laboratory and the operations centre by sealing off tunnels and rebuilding barricades. It is their only chance.

Then we see Ripley with Hicks for a moment. He gives her a wristband – it's a locator signal, in case of trouble. She smiles and thanks him, and he says it doesn't mean they're engaged or anything. This is the first valuable, adult bond Ripley has had in the two films so far.

And it equips her further, for now we see her carrying Newt into a quiet part of the operations centre, where she has made up a bed for the exhausted child. But Newt is afraid of bad dreams. She says that her mother always told her there weren't real monsters – but there are. 'Why do they tell kids that?' Ripley gives her the wrist locator. But the child doesn't want the woman to leave her. I'll be in the next room, says Ripley. I'm not going to leave you – that's a promise. The child pushes her further, and Ripley adds, Cross my heart and hope to die. They embrace. As so often in James Cameron's films, in crises a strange family strength emerges.

'Now, go to sleep,' says Ripley, aware of the irony, 'and don't dream.'

15

A little later, we are in the medical laboratory. Bishop is telling Ripley what he has learned from the species. The acidic blood oxidises once it is exposed to air. Ripley questions him, and they agree that the alien needs a human body for incubation and development – one egg, one human. But what is laying the eggs? asks Ripley. 'Something we haven't seen yet,' Bishop speculates.

She tells Bishop to destroy the specimen as soon as he's finished his work.

The bright, shining eye of the artificial person widens. Mr Burke has given him instructions to keep them – he was very specific.

At which point, Burke himself enters the conversation. He tells Ripley that the specimens are worth millions. Get them back to Earth, and they'll both be set up.

She tells him, 'You're crazy, Burke, do you know that?' And then she turns on him with a vengeance, blaming him for the death of all 157 colonists. She has found the colony's log and established by an order of 6/12/79 (is that 1979 or 2079?) that Burke himself gave the order for setting up the colony – when he had reason to believe there were aliens on LV426.

He admits it was a mistake. She holds him and shakes him, and promises to have him disgraced. For were those colonists not fed to the monsters? He tells her he expected more from her.

'I'm happy to disappoint you,' she says.

16

The situation worsens. Bishop has noted venting coming from the processing plant. There must have been damage during the battle. He now expects it to explode in about four hours, with a 30-kilometre blast radius. It's a process that can't be averted or shut down. Hudson begins to panic again. Ripley says that there is another shuttle on the ship – the *Sulaco*, it is called now* – if they could bring it down by remote. But their transmitter was destroyed in the APC. There is a transmitter in the colony, but it's badly damaged – at the moment, its dish cannot be aligned. It would take someone to go out and do the work, in great jeopardy from the aliens. 'I'll do it,' says Bishop. 'I'll go.' There is a lovely shot of his wizened face, the eyes increasingly alive and even wry. I'd rather not, he admits. 'I may be synthetic, but I'm not stupid.'

Bishop has found a conduit that leads to the transmitter. It is so cramped that the 180-metre journey will take him forty minutes. An

*Sulaco is the 'twilight country' in which Conrad set much of *Nostromo*.

hour to do the work. Thirty minutes to prep the ship. Fifty minutes' flight time. It could not be closer. 'Good luck,' says Ripley; she has found a way to appreciate androids at last. And Bishop drops down into the conduit. There is a vivid shot as he begins the journey, hunched over, the arrowhead of his face savagely illuminated by his flashlight, inching towards the camera. We see the far pinpoint of light from his point of view.

17

Hicks alerts Hudson and Vasquez – 'Stay frosty' – so as to let no alien inside their perimeter. But he suggests to Ripley that she try to sleep. Instead, she asks him to make sure she doesn't end up like one of the cocooned colonists. He responds by introducing her to an M-41 pulse rifle with a grenade launcher. Show me how it works, she asks. He stops short of the grenade launcher, but she tells him she can handle herself. 'Yeah, I noticed,' he says.

Carrying her new gun, Ripley heads for the medical laboratory and meets Gorman. He is conscious again, with a white bandage around his head. He tries to apologise to her, but she won't hear it. Instead, she goes into the lab and finds that Newt's bed is empty. The child is asleep on the floor. Ripley lies down and prepares to sleep beside her.

We cut outside to the windswept planet and to that other member of the 'family', Bishop, who is now working at the transmitter. At last, he gets the dish to move, and he taps in the message 'ENABLE', which begins to prepare the second shuttle on board the ship, the *Sulaco*. We see it move into launch position.

Ripley is suddenly awake. Lying on the floor, she sees a couple of glass containers on their sides, rolling together, and clinking. She wakes Newt and tells her to be quiet. But as she stands up, one of the small aliens – of the size that got Kane – jumps her. It goes for her head, but she throws it aside. Her gun is not on the bed where she put it. She tries to open the doors, but they are locked. She sees her gun in the next room. She waves at the TV camera, trying to attract Hicks's attention. We see her image on the screen, and a frozen-faced Burke watching. But he turns away and declines to notice. She picks up a chair and tries to smash through the heavy glass.

Finally, she goes to the sprinklers and turns on a lighter so that the fire alarm system sounds. Hicks is alerted, and he and the others come running to help. But the alien has struck at Ripley again: it has a tail round her throat, and its many fingers are desperate to get at her face, her mouth. Ripley is struggling for her life against a visceral terror.

Hicks shoots at the glass to weaken it and then hurls himself through. Hudson is attacked by a second monster, and he is able to kill it. Hicks helps pull the alien from Ripley, and Vasquez kills it.

Ripley knows it was Burke's plot. He must have freed the live specimens in the hope that they would impregnate Ripley and Newt, thus allowing some version of the creature to get home. He denies it. 'This is so nuts – it's paranoid delusion.' Ripley tells him she's not sure which species is worse.

Whereupon the lights go out.

18

'They cut the power,' says Ripley – here is yet another tribute to the malign intelligence of the aliens, though why didn't they sever the power lines earlier? What follows is shot in a kind of infra-red light. Hudson is recording movement inside the perimeter – 'Movement all over the place.' They seal the door to their inner room, but the readings on the sensor indicate a presence inside the room. Ripley realises that the creatures must be above the ceiling. Hudson pushes up a panel, turns his flashlight, and sees the grinning, leering parade of aliens advancing. The Marines fire at the ceiling, and some of the creatures jump down on them. A lurid fire-fight lights up the infra-red.

Ripley kills one monster: we see it fragmenting in the blast of the pulse rifle. The coils of another alien grasp Hudson's leg and pull him down. Vasquez holds off the creatures as the others make for the medical laboratory. But Burke has taken refuge there, sealing the doors, until he finds he has company: a large alien that strikes at the very man who was so anxious to preserve the new species. There is not even time or the light for a look at the surprise on Burke's face.

In the emergency, Ripley leads Newt, Hicks and Gorman into the ventilator system, with the resolute Vasquez still protecting their rear. Newt knows these corridors, and she leads their retreat. On the run, Hicks radios to Bishop, who tells him the shuttle is due in sixteen minutes.

Backing off down the ventilator system, Vasquez lets one creature come so close that when she kills it she is crippled by the scalding acid. Gorman goes back to help her. She sees who it is, and grunts, 'You always were an asshole, Gorman', but when he unpins the grenade, she embraces him and the explosion that unites them. They take out a couple of monsters in this last display of Marine spirit.

Which leaves Ripley, Newt, Hicks and Bishop.

19

We are in the era of combat now, a merciless, close-quartered, running engagement that *Aliens* has always promised, and of which Vasquez has been the outstanding exponent. But she is gone, in an exultant act of heroism that makes the body a bomb – as so often in the *Alien* films, the body becomes the fundamental unit and sign of meaning. Combat in the film is the martial montage of muzzles gasping flame, the sounds of firing, the shattering of the aliens, and their screeching. The whole thing is obvious, not far from automatic, but compulsive, interlocking and as inescapable as sex, once begun. The threat – of jaws within jaws, snapping at the lens itself – is hideous: viewers of *Alien* films often feel the need to shower away the gluey mucous of the creatures afterwards. The surge of power in the pulse rifles and the flame-throwers is enough to enlist the most insistent pacifist. For combat on film *is* like sex: it is a joining rhythm and the chance of crescendo. And as we participate in the blazing away of it all, even fear lifts a little. We are close here to some inner secret about weapons, about how they appeal to the id while putting away idiot consequences.

And so, the very blast of the explosion that takes out Vasquez, Gorman and a couple of aliens billows down the vent system and blows tiny Newt off her insecure hold on a revolving spindle. Hicks and Ripley do all they can to save her. They thrust a gun into the spokes of the spindle to jam it. Ripley reaches down a hand to clutch Newt's jacket – but the child, obeying Hitchcockian laws of physics, slips out of the garment and slides away down a steel chute.

Ripley and Hicks follow her, tracking on the wrist signal she wears. But we see that Newt is up to her chest, clutching her doll, Casey, in a great pool. She hears their cries, climbs up on some piping and pushes her fingers through the grating above (this is *Third Man* stuff – you cannot do chase-and-action movies without respecting the past, except by adding inventiveness in violence and cruelty). Hicks starts to cut through the grating, to get at Newt. But the movement sensors tell them aliens are coming, and in a moment – at Newt's level – we see the Loch Nessy form of one surfacing behind her. She screams, and the scream is like fire; it is another way of wiping away the image with uncertainty. By the time Hicks gets through there is nothing but the plastic head of Casey floating on the water, her eyelids pushed open and shut by the wash of disturbed water.

'She's alive!' insists Ripley, against the immediate evidence, yet clinging to the deeper laws of movie suspense and motherly dedication. They run back to the elevator, and as they are waiting for the doors to close, an alien thrusts itself at them. Hicks fires and kills it, but the dire yellow acid spills on his armour and burns ragged holes in it. He is wounded.

They emerge from the elevator, with Ripley supporting Hicks, and stagger to the transmitter site where Bishop is bringing in the precious shuttle. He tells them they have twenty-six minutes left: he is like a godsend, and a referee, vital to the game.

'We're not leaving,' says Ripley.

'We're not?' is Bishop's reply – he never will quite get people.

They carry Hicks on board the shuttle. Bishop pilots the craft towards the processing plant, while Ripley outfits herself from the shuttle armoury with flame-throwers and grenades. Bishop finds a landing platform, amid blue arcs of electricity. The plant is heating up already. Ripley loads up a belt of grenades. Bishop tells her that in nineteen minutes the whole thing will be a cloud of vapour the size of Nebraska. She orders Hicks not to let Bishop leave, and sets off to rescue Newt.

20

There is extraordinary assurance in *Aliens* at this point, and it hardly countenances a chance of Ripley losing. That drive is deeply stirring, yet it is not typical of the series' ambiguity. No matter the peril they are in, this is a moment of glory for the film's oddly assorted family. They rise above every travail, as confident as Hallmark's Christmas.

Ripley takes the elevator down, still loading her guns as she goes, against the warning voice of the emergency system. The claxon sounds, and throbs; there are fourteen minutes left to ensure escape. Ripley tosses aside her jacket, and puts on a harness over her singlet with the flame-thrower slung over one shoulder.

She gets out of the elevator at ground level and uses the wrist sensor as a direction-finder. As she moves forward, she blasts the corridors or tunnels ahead with her cleansing flame-thrower. The beeper's sound quickens and becomes nearly a single note. Whereupon, Ripley finds the discarded wrist sensor in a bed of slime. She feels anguish – the sense of bereavement for the loss of a child.

We cut away to find Newt in a cocoon. The child's eye sees an alien egg open in front of her, and then the hatched arm beginning to crawl over the lip of the pod. She screams. And Ripley hears. She runs towards the sound, blasts the new claw and pulls Newt from her sticky cocoon. At which point, fires start to break out in the plant.

Carrying Newt, Ripley edges away and then stops when she realises that she is surrounded by alien eggs – she has reached the core of their kingdom. And the life-giving force is a great membrane trunk that dribbles succour into the eggs. She traces that trunk backwards and finds it is attached to the largest of the aliens, awesome in articulation, looming above her, its limbs spread out like a fan, its head a great hood. It shows Ripley her jaws. It is the Queen. Her courtiers are in the shadows surrounding Ripley, waiting to attack.

And now Ripley's hard, practical intelligence rises to the challenge. Holding the Queen's attention, she demonstrates the flame-thrower and then points it at the eggs. We see Ripley's face, as from above, cold and unequivocal, cruel even, one new mother daring another. The Queen drops her head and backs away; the courtier aliens make the same movement, clearing the way. And so Ripley, holding Newt's hand, makes her withdrawal. But then, by chance, another egg opens. Ripley sees it, cocks her head, and then turns the flame-thrower on the eggs, bathing them in fire. The Queen screeches in betrayal and wretchedness. She was not quite as intricate, or as subtly malign, as Ripley. Humans have their edge.

Whereupon, Ripley torches every alien she can see and fires grenades into their soft mass until acid spills out. As she and Newt escape, she throws her harness of grenades into the fire, and there is a fierce explosion.

They reach the elevator. The warning voice gives them four minutes. They get in the elevator and shoot at another alien through the mesh covering. With two minutes left, they come out of the elevator and find no shuttle. Ripley cries out to Bishop in despair. Her flame-thrower is empty. Explosions begin to rock the plant.

Then another elevator arrives at the top floor and one more alien gets out.

'Close your eyes, baby,' Ripley tells Newt. But Bishop in the shuttle rises up behind her, out of the flames. They scramble aboard. Bishop directs the shuttle at the last alien, destroying it, before he blasts off. 'Hey, we made it,' Ripley tells Newt, and the child says, 'I knew you'd come.' Ripley has earned trust. And as the shuttle escapes, the great blue in the white light of extinguishing explosion wells up behind them.

21

Just as victory is certain, so no one by now would overlook the tradition of the alien's last play.

We are back on the *Sulaco*. Hicks is on drugs to relieve his pain, but Bishop reckons he will recover. They are in the loading dock area, where Ripley, whole-heartedly, wants to thank and congratulate Bishop for what he did. He apologises that he left his post, but things were becoming so unstable.

'Bishop,' she says, and she has learned this, 'you did OK.'

'I did?' he asks. (It was Henriksen's idea to make Bishop feel fourteen.)

He seems uncommonly touched, but the piercing is something more: it's the great tail of one last alien, emerging like a spear from his chest. His mouth froths with white liquid. He is hoisted up where one further alien – is it the Queen? – severs his legs from his upper body and throws the chest and the head down on the ground like a soiled shirt.

Then the alien prepares to get Ripley and Newt. But Ripley attracts the beast's attention while Newt scurries under the floor, and so the impatient demon prowls over the grid, sending whiplash tails and clawed arms into every possible entrance-way. Meanwhile, Ripley shuts herself in a sealed compartment – doing what?

The answer is not long in coming. The doors open again, and there is Ripley, inserted in the huge mechanical loader with which she was so deft before. A light behind gives a comic, silhouetted look to the weird spiderman, as she advances for final combat. 'Get away from her, you bitch!' she roars at the alien – it is one of the great lines in the series, and an inspiration to many women viewers. Maternal fondness, or sweetness, is a stock-in-trade of the American movie, and one that easily supports male notions of superiority. It is so much rarer to see the energy, the ferocity, and the willingness to die for the child in mothers – for those things may daunt the male fantasy.

Ripley uses the ponderous arms to jab and hook the alien, just like Robinson schooling the unruly La Motta in his own lack of skill. The monster tries to get in at her, but this Ripley is his match. As she fights, she opens a hatch in the floor, so that a large cube of space is made available. Then she gets the alien in her two arms and prepares to dump it in the hold. But the alien is not a novice, and it hooks on to one of her flat feet and drags her down with it.

But the weight of the loader pins the alien and Ripley extricates herself so that she can climb up the ladder to safety. Even so, as she moves up, a coil whips around her foot and holds her. So Ripley hits the reachable switch and opens the bottom floor panel of the hold, letting in the great suck of space.

Above her, on the floor of the deck, Newt and the fragment of Bishop are blown like scraps of paper. But he gets a hold on the grid and then keeps another hand to save the child. And, despite the great gale, Ripley holds on as both the loader and the alien tumble out into space. She hauls herself up and closes off the floor again. 'Not bad for a human,' say the remains of Bishop.

There is a cut and we are in a secured *Sulaco*, sailing 'home' – but will we ever get there? Ripley has put the wounded Hicks and the shreds of Bishop in the sleeping coffins. Now she tucks Newt in. Will we sleep? Newt asks, and can I dream? Yes, Ripley smiles, though she is by now a little too old and battle-weary for such ease. Nevertheless, one of the greatest action films ever made ends and settles on the sight of two faces – mother and child – in their side-by-side sleeping bays, trusting the future.

Interlude

'This time it's war,' said the posters for *Aliens*, and nobody disputed the concentrated grip of James Cameron's combat scenes, the mounting firepower, the dread sense of enemy or the feeling of a work that belonged in the tradition of Marine movies* – even if these Marines were wiped out nearly to a man and woman, or if victory depended on the stirring resolution of a woman and the remains of a robot. But *Aliens* was much more, just as James Cameron has proved himself not simply a master of narrative and technology. He has a simple but deep affection for family ties that was evident even in *The Terminator* and which gave *Aliens* a new emotional energy. Above all, Ripley was able to seem like a mother and the centre of an unexpected family unit. The power and terror of the aliens had been countered by the way a few people made themselves into a team more resilient than the Corps mentality.

The critics responded. In *Newsweek*, David Ansen praised Cameron for 'playing it straight. No arched eyebrow here, no self-conscious old movie references. Just back-to-basics good storytelling . . . For sheer intensity, the final forty-five minutes of *Aliens* is not likely to be matched by any movie soon.'

---

*The John Wayne classic, *Sands of Iwo Jima* (1949), is the flag in that tradition – but the ethos goes all the way through *Pride of the Marines* (1945) and *Battle Cry* (1955) to Jack Nicholson and his boys in *A Few Good Men* (1992). Thus it goes from real combat to aggressive attitude, and a nearly fascist sense of virtue.

The picture drew in domestic rentals in its first run of $42.5 million. It was the fifth best earner of the year, behind *Top Gun*, *The Karate Kid, Part II*, *Crocodile Dundee* and *Star Trek IV: The Long Voyage Home*. Effectively, therefore, it did the business of the original film, and that was akin to a disappointment. *Alien* is far more atmospheric and less active than *Aliens*. The second film had more attractive people: from its outset, Ripley is a sympathetic figure, a complete heroine; then there is Newt, the fear over survival, and the team spirit. *Aliens* was still counted a success (though it was actually less profitable at home just because of the increased budget). Yet maybe, already, it and its monsters had lost that vital bit of magic – their novelty. Nothing in *Aliens* was talked about in the way of the beast that had burst out of John Hurt's chest.

Still, the second movie had an extra claim for respectability. Among its seven Oscar nominations, Sigourney Weaver got a best actress nod for Ripley. The departure in this was not fully recognised at the time, for in the entire history of Oscar, no actress had ever been nominated in an action film, a sci-fi movie or a horror picture. (The closest to it was Faye Dunaway in *Bonnie and Clyde*.) Few people (herself included) thought Weaver would win – her rivals were Kathleen Turner in *Peggy Sue Got Married*, Sissy Spacek in *Crimes of the Heart*, Jane Fonda in *The Morning After*, and, the eventual winner, Marlee Matlin in *Children of a Lesser God*. But the distinction was a tribute not just to the actress, but to Cameron's re-directing of the series. The adrenalin rush had felt very satisfying this time. As he would in *Titanic*, Cameron had found the right balance of spectacle, sensation and ordinary emotional involvement. Indeed, if audiences were growing bored with the aliens – or coming to terms with their terror – they might be becoming more attached to Ripley. It was a lesson lost in the next few years.

There were other nominations: for art direction, for sound, for James Horner's score, for editing – and two actual victories: to Don Sharpe for sound effects editing; and to Robert Skotak, Stan Winston, John Richardson and Suzanne Benson for visual effects.

Fox and Brandywine wanted to seize the day: a third movie should come quicker than the second. The project that became *Alien³* was aimed originally at an opening in the spring of 1990. Not long after *Aliens* opened, David Giler happened to read William Gibson's cyberpunk novel *Neuromancer*. He showed the book to Walter Hill and suggested that Gibson was just the fresh vision they needed on the series. And so the novelist was hired – though he had never written a screenplay before – and given a twelve-page story treatment by Giler and Hill in which the Company was battling an ill-defined radical socialist spacecraft (also from Earth) with alien eggs as the ultimate prize.

Gibson had liked *Alien* very much – 'I think it influenced my prose SF writing because it was the first funked-up, dirty kitchen sink spaceship and it made a big impression on me.' In talks with Giler and Hill, Gibson was struck by the enthusiasm with which the two producers now speculated over the deeper meanings of the series – whether the aliens were best read as a symbol of cancer, or of HIV, for instance. There were blue-sky dreams about a third film that would explain the origins of the aliens and chart the future of mankind. Still, as much as Brandywine longed for freshness, something new, and an infinitely ambitious range, the new film needed to give audiences what they had enjoyed in the first two. Gibson said: 'They had a choice between opening this thing up and expanding the meaning of the first two films or going for closure. They went for closure.' As in any movie sequel writing, everyone asks for something the same and something different at once.

Gibson did what he could to tie up loose ends: his script had Newt going back to Earth to live with her grandparents, and it gave a continuing role to Hicks. But he admitted that his script was very moody and rather arty, if only because he was a novice at film writing. Giler and Hill were not happy, and they hoped to get Gibson to revise his draft while working with their chosen director, Renny Harlin (the director of *Nightmare on Elm Street 4*). However, Gibson said he preferred not to pursue the subject (if Gibson promised new ideas, Harlin was a move towards raw action), and so Eric Red was hired as the next writer. He had written several scripts in the general sci-fi/horror area – notably, *Near Dark* and *The Hitcher* – and he had just made his directorial debut with *Body Parts* (about a murderer's body parts grafted on to other people).

Red met several problems as he was asked to start again from the Giler-Hill treatment. First, Giler and Hill were not available for him. But they did now indicate that they weren't sure whether Sigourney Weaver would be in the third film – and this seemed to be because they had lost interest in her. The actress was growing older – and more proprietorial. She would request a lot more money; yet, in some eyes, her central role restricted the development of more action. This matter is clouded, to say the least. But there were difficulties again between Fox and the profit participants as to whether or not the distributor was reporting full earnings on *Aliens*. As late as 1992, according to Sigourney Weaver, Fox were saying that *Aliens* was still in the red. Eventually, Brandywine, James Cameron and Weaver took action together against Fox that was settled privately.

At any event, Eric Red was trying to invent a new leading character: a Special Services commando. He also envisaged a new kind of alien that changed its form at will to suit circumstances. Again, no one liked the result. Giler called it 'absolutely dreadful' and Ms Weaver noticed that Ripley was missing! David Twohy was the next writer in line (he would come to be the writer on *The Fugitive*, and one of many writers on *Waterworld*), and he pursued the notion of a Company ship at odds with a Soviet spacecraft. He dealt with the Weaver problem by having a central character who could be a man or a woman, and he made this significant contribution: a planet that was serving as a prison.

But matters took another turn when Renny Harlin announced that he had lost faith in the venture. He said the writers had delivered only 'a tired carbon copy' of the first two movies. (His future would consist of *Die Hard 2*, *The Adventures of Ford Fairlane*, *Cliffhanger* and *Cutthroat*

Island.) By now, in late 1988 or early 1989, the project had incurred heavy development costs while getting nowhere. Harlin, Twohy, Red and Gibson would all have been paid and paid off, and those fees help to build the budget of any eventual picture. Fox chairman, Joe Roth, let it be known that he couldn't imagine an *Alien* picture without Ripley.

Still, Giler and Hill then took what was their boldest step: they hired the young New Zealander, Vincent Ward, whose film *The Navigator* had caused a stir at festivals. Subtitled 'A Medieval Odyssey', *The Navigator* concerned a child in the England of the Middle Ages. To avoid the Black Death, he digs a tunnel – and emerges in a 1988 city. Tolkien-like, it is an inspired and utterly original movie with a unique visual style. Choosing Ward was exactly the kind of gamble on talent that Hollywood is supposed to flinch from *and* the daring impulse that still existed within the commercial machinations on the *Alien* franchise.

Ward saw no script worth persisting with, so he elected to begin again, with John Fasano (who had written *Another 48 Hrs*). As one might have expected, he and his writer came up with something startlingly inventive and complete. His film was to take place on a tiny planet, Arceon, the home of a colony of banished monks who were still living as if in the Middle Ages. Ripley arrives, with wild tales of the monster, and the monster in turn is regarded by the monks as a possible second coming of the Black Death. Ripley fights the beast with Brother John, Abbot of the community, and another android. Ward liked Twohy's notion of aliens that could take different forms – his could be a sheep (all very well), or a field of corn, or a sheet of glass! Moreover, Ward reintroduced H. R. Giger to the project – an outcast on *Aliens*, and rather sulky because of it. Did I add that, at the end of his story, Ward wanted every single character dead? And he wanted a world in which wood was the only building material. But how did the wood get there?

This picture may be one of the great unmade projects of our time:

the clash of the Middle Ages and the future is rich in prospect; the image of aliens wreaking havoc in a field of Brueghel or Bosch only adds to it; and Ward's story is coherent and vital, even if it seems to treat Ripley as not much more than an instrument. But Ward was not a Hollywood person. He did not always make the ritual, polite concessions to power that are in order before tyranny has its moment. He made it clear that he would not be needing Stan Winston or John Richardson. He was a little on the arrogant side.

Walter Hill fired Ward (not without regrets), and the New Zealander took yet another pay-off as he went away to make *Map of the Human Heart*, another entirely personal and visionary picture about an Eskimo boy taken to the civilised world. But Giler and Hill had liked Ward's script enough to hire David Fincher as their next director with instructions to 'simplify' Ward's script but to persist with it. Fincher was twenty-seven; he had never made a film; but he had a terrific reputation from commercials and music videos. And so he worked with one more writer, Larry Ferguson, to get a script. Their collaboration was not fruitful – Sigourney Weaver said that Ferguson made Ripley 'sound like this uptight camp counsellor who swears every other minute'. Nevertheless, Ferguson offered enough suggestions that were used for him to qualify for an eventual screen credit.

Finally, Giler and Hill determined that they would have to write the script themselves. They converted the monastery back into a prison and delivered a script by the end of 1990 – that left Fox cool. And so Rex Pickett came in to do rewrites with Fincher. It was only in December 1990 that Sigourney Weaver belatedly signed on to play Ripley (for $5.5 million – she was determined not to be screwed again) – and production was supposed to start at Pinewood on January 14th, 1991! Moreover, because of the tightness of these negotiations, Weaver's script ideas were being absorbed into the work-in-progress: she was against Ripley having any guns this time. Giler and Hill came back (at Weaver's insistence), and they now found – at the end of everything – that they were rewriting in a desperate effort to stay ahead of the shooting. Weaver was past forty now – that dangerous age. Her career had peaked with *Gorillas in the Mist* and *Working Girl*. But she was hardly secure; and she was married now with a child. She wanted a great film *and* a reassuring salary: she hoped the one meant the other.

And so *Alien³* came to be made, as almost a classic example of how not to do it. A novice director had a script still being hacked out that retained elements from several previous and distinct drafts. David Fincher would go on to prove himself (with *Seven* and *The Game*), and under the circumstances it may be that *Alien³* has more integrity than anyone had a right to expect. But the picture was out of control, and the budget was now close to $50 million.

Something like an alliance formed between Fincher and Weaver. She said she loved the prospect of Ripley being bald, and she sometimes defended the young director against the studio: 'The [audience] is going to expect guns, action nonstop and David has done something very stylish, cynical, yet innocent at the same time. Maybe some people will say it's too slow or existential. And that's got people at Fox a little nervous.' Maybe being rich at last urged her to be more daring and self-effacing?

No one supported the passing of Ripley more than Sigourney Weaver. 'I know it sounds crazy,' she said, 'but I came to realise that the only way she could finally get any peace was if I, the actress, were willing to go deep into the material and allow her a release.' In many ways, the actress had become the *auteur*, defying anyone else to know the story better than she did. But not every knowing actress has the detachment to tell her story clearly.

The alien effects were put in the hands of Tom Woodruff, Jr and Alec Gillis, who had been assistants to Stan Winston on *Aliens*. Alex Thomson handled the photography and helped define a dark, sour look that Fincher would extend on *Seven*. The only other surviving character from the series was the android Bishop – though, arguably,

Bishop is one of the great coups of the film. Hicks and Newt would be killed off. Otherwise, a group of English actors – nearly all with shaved heads – were chosen to be the prisoners. Giger did drawings for *Alien³*, though it is far from certain that they were ever used. Indeed, they had been commissioned as an aide to story development. Giger was vocal about Fox's cost-cutting – no matter that this third film would cost more than one and two together. 'Imagine', he said, 'what could have been possible if all that money [Weaver's salary] had been spent on the creature!'

Trailers appeared for *Alien³* in the spring of 1991. But the film was not ready on time. There was reshooting in November 1991 and re-editing until very near to actual release, in the spring of 1992. 'The Bitch is Back!' the posters said then, with all the threadbare confidence of a character who tells you that all the aliens are dead now.

ALIEN³

1

Nothing about *Alien³* encourages us to be of good cheer. It is not simply a movie that gives audiences none of the things they might expect or want; it also deprives them of elements they liked and remembered. Yet no one could accuse Part 3 of being a mindless exploitation of the series. No. 3 was new, different, sombre and seemingly final. It was as if, somehow, the story had been entrusted to a film-maker who would leave no remains for any further sequel. To that extent, commercially, No. 3 was both self-destructive and drastically innovative, faithful to the tradition only to the extent that it let it run its darkly logical course. To go on, after this No. 3, would require prodigious insight and enterprise. Nothing less than greatness would suffice, and nothing less than engagement with spiritual and intellectual questions hitherto only flirted with.

As the 20th Century-Fox fanfare introduces the picture, so its last chords are flattened and prolonged, as if the music were screaming. (But is it asking for help, or warning us to stay away?)

We see space, amber near the top of the screen, deep blue below. Then the credits are broken up by brief views of the story. So we see two faces in the cryogenic sleeping compartments, though it is not easy to identify them. We see the hull of the ship passing by with the lettering *U.S.S. Sulaco*. And then, with terrible directness, a shot that pans over empty racks on board the ship and comes to rest on the end of the trunk that we may recall feeding the eggs in *Aliens*. That appendage is dripping. This is, or was, the Queen, and it is a passenger on the *Sulaco*.

That glimpse is swift, and many watching *Alien³* might not have recollected it, but the next shot leaves no doubt: it is a low-angle view of the spindly fingers of the alien's 'hand', or claw, stretching and reaching out. The next shot, very quick, sees that hand reaching towards one of the faces in the sleeping compartments. And in the next, we see a face beneath the glass – Ripley's – and hear the glass crack, like ice stepped on by a heavy boot. Then drops of fluid fall on a white floor, and eat away at it. Rising smoke meets a detector system.

A computer screen comes alive. A female voice says, 'Stasis inter-rupted'. An alarm system begins. We see a face in a cryogenic compartment, stirring. And then an X-ray of the hand enveloping a human head. There are red warning lights and sirens. There is an explosion and a fireball. The sleeping coffin slides into a chute. Wheels lock into place. We see the face of Ripley, disturbed. And then a portion of the *Sulaco* is ejected and drifting, spinning towards a new planet. In what resembles a daylight shot – the first of the series? – albeit an overcast, storm-heavy day, much more Magritte than Monet, this falling craft plunges into the grey sea off a shore where derricks stand like skeletons. The title comes up: 'Fiorina Fury 161, Outer Veil Mineral Ore, Double Y Chromosome Work Correctional Facility, Maximum Security.'

2

Audiences are not accustomed to being so vanquished, or under-mined, in a credit sequence. So, many may not have 'seen' or weighed the dread theorem of those fragments. They may have preferred to read the credit sequence as a vague preview, no matter its miserly exactitude. But to any follower of the series there is little doubt but that the *Sulaco* was, from the outset, penetrated by the Queen alien (the greatest of them all and the one with a sense of vengeance to settle with Ripley). We heard the crack when the thick glass broke; it could have been a spine going, or a small tree, and as the nicked alien bled a little on the floor, surely its grasp enclosed Ripley's face, and . . . made her his or its? Or let us say, 'compromised' the lofty, pugnacious Lieutenant, the lovely woman who found such maternal strength in *Aliens*. But if from the start suspense and hope are taken away, then surely we require large things to fill their place?

3

There is a blast and the hatch on the shuttle falls in – its removal lets a mass of raw white light into the interior. There are men looking in. They are rough, hairless, dressed in makeshift, drab clothes; they give no promise of a refined world. They have a barking dog with them, a heavy brown, mongrelised retriever with a domed skull. One man peers in. He estimates three, maybe four, people. A voice outside says, 'Hurry, it will soon be 40 below.' Then the investigator shouts that one's still alive, and we see Ripley's head moving inside her coffin.

Whereupon, we begin to see an inventory of the passengers on the shuttle, their pictures and basic information coming up on a video screen (we gather later that this data is not known on Fiorina – it must be being reported at Company headquarters) and we are about to learn something intimate, touching and romantic, even if it is too late. Ripley's first name is Ellen: there it is, with her number – 95156170 – and a photograph of her from a time before we knew her.

And as we reassess this heroine, we see her from above, a long brown body in a soiled grey singlet and pants, being lifted on to a bed, or a gurney. There is an oxygen mask being applied to her, though she tries feebly to push it away.

On the computer, we see the fact: a little girl is listed, approximately twelve years old – DEAD.

Then Corporal Dwayne Hicks on the screen – DEAD. We see him in his coffin, a spike apparently driven through his body.

And Bishop, a 341-B with NEGATIVE CAPABILITY. We see his shattered torso, with plastic sheeting over it, flapping in the great wind.

Ripley is being further examined. There are something like fingerprints on her face – as if from where she was gripped.

The dog barks, trying to get into the wrecked interior, and we see an alien flexing in a corner of the ceiling, the beast biding its time.

We cut to what looks like a large hall in a nineteenth-century factory, with galleries rising above it. White light falls downwards on the bald head and Yorkshire strut of Andrews, superintendent of this prison. He is portly, self-important, stupid but sly: he is the excellent Brian Glover as a jumped-up provincial civil servant. His prison looks Dickensian: the inmates are shabby, eccentric, startling characters who share in a kind of subdued, oppressed state. Spurning self-pity, or hope, utterly content as dregs and dross.

'This is Rumour Control,' says Andrews. 'Here are the facts.' He tells the assembly that a vehicle crashed, and the survivor is a woman. There is widespread concern at this, for the prisoners have taken a vow of celibacy. They hate the idea of their own unexpected opportunity. A man who is clearly not fully a part of the community, Clemens (Charles Dance), watches wryly. A forceful black prisoner, Dillon (Charles S. Dutton), interprets the mood – he seems like a leader: no one wants a violation of their harmony, he says.

Andrews assures them all that he has requested a rescue team to remove the woman – 'ASAP'. He asks Clemens about her health. He replies that she is unconscious, but not doing badly – 'She'll live.' Andrews orders that she must be confined to the infirmary, and he urges the inmates, more like their clergyman than their warder, 'Gentlemen, we should all stick to our set routines.' As if order (or barrenness) had any chance in this blasted place now.

4

Her name is Ellen? Ellen. For two whole films Ripley went without benefit or burden of 'Ellen'. She could pretend to herself that she was a good soldier, one of the guys – after all, she never argued when the horribly experienced child, Rebecca, said that she went by the name of Newt now, as if everyone had had to give up that much feminine

identity to become an underground creature. But in learning that
Ripley was an Ellen, we understand the profound absence of ordinary
romance, sexual possibility, or even contact in *Alien³*. This is a time in
the history of the human race when such things are less considered,
or fancied. There's the nub of it: in coming almost casually upon the
name Ellen we realise how much of inner life has been put aside or
abandoned.

So, Ellen Ripley once was . . . well, the tense-looking but rather
puppy-fat girl in her I.D. picture. Ellen? Not Eleanor or Helen. Just
Ellen. The daughter of a soldier, maybe, an A-student at the military
academy. A rather awkward, fierce, over-tall teenage girl, from
rural Oregon, Nebraska or Vermont, someone who banked a lot
of self-sacrifice on getting to be proficient, respected, respectable.
But someone who may have longed to be noticed, treated tenderly,
and whispered to as 'Ellen'. Did Ellen Ripley ever wear a dress, do
you think, after she was fourteen or fifteen? Did she fuck around
the way young soldiers are supposed to do, if only to avoid ever
falling in love? Has Ellen ever been in love? It is a different kind
of question once we know about 'Ellen', once we know she is not
just Judy, plain Priscilla, lovely Lucy, or even aspiring Sigourney.
So that name comes as a belated, nearly a posthumous gift: there is
a kind of cruelty in it, as well as the recognition of inwardness. It's
like finding an old, unexpected love letter in your mother's drawer,
on going through her faded, forsaken things after her death. If only
you had known earlier, you might have known she was knowable.
If you'd realised Ripley was Ellen you could have asked her out.

And yet, so much is taken away. In *Aliens*, though no bond was
ever forged in law or sex, we had gathered a family: Ripley had
adopted Newt, and promised never to leave her; Hicks had given
Ripley a wrist-band with the gruff soldierly laconicism that they
weren't engaged or anything, just star-crossed lovers; and Bishop
had made himself invaluably heroic and altruistic, those qualities
so few real humans ever get. But now Ripley is plunged in triple

mourning: she has lost all of them, as if loss must be the continuity in the series.

Of course she does not quite know this yet. She is struggling back to consciousness. But we know it, and it is one more crushing proof that *Alien³* does not mean to be kind to us. This story will not repeat the half-legendary way, in the *Terminator* films, that a broken family repairs the world's history. Within a matter of moments, the surgent power of prowess and trial by ordeal that marks *Aliens* is wiped away. Life as that film knew it counts for so little now – so learning 'Ellen' has come too late.

5

We are in the infirmary. Ripley is asleep, or unconscious, and Clemens is watching her. He has a crew-cut of hair, and Charles Dance's bleak, kind eyes. He is preparing a syringe for her, and he does it with care, and even affection. He is fond of his needle. But as he is about to put it in the pit of her elbow, her free hand reaches out to prevent him. 'What's that?' she demands.

Her inner alertness surprises him. But he is quiet and wordy in his answer. He likes to talk, and he has not lost the art, even if no one else on Fiorina deserves it. 'Just a little cocktail of my own invention,' he says. 'An eye-opener?'

She wonders if he is a doctor, and he dodges the question slightly by saying 'Chief Medical Officer'. Not that he has any assistants. She weakens, or trusts him, and he slips the cocktail in.

Ripley does not look good. There is bruising around and above her left eye, and a cut on that eyebrow. Nothing explains it. But we have to wonder whether the alien's grip was especially severe there, full of torque, like a spinner's grip on the seam. The eye itself seems a little wider open and more bloodshot than it should be.

Clemens tells her that he ought to shave her head. There is a problem of lice on Fiorina – further evidence that it has not really advanced beyond a Dickensian state of existence. He'll give her clippers so that she can attend to her private parts.

She asks what happened to the others, and he says they didn't make it – Dance can effortlessly get the tone of a squadron leader during the Battle of Britain. This is not easy news to react to, for the character or the actress. Ripley is in the military; she has worked hard for that stiff upper lip. And Weaver is plainly intelligent in a way that doesn't reckon on women being over-emotional. I once heard a director say – someone who had tested Ms Weaver for a key role – that she didn't cry well, or naturally. Her Ripley looks stricken here; yet the feeling is intelligently conveyed – it does not rise helplessly from within.

Ripley *is* thinking. She has to go look at the ship, she says; she stands up – naked, although we don't see it – and says she's ready to go like that. Clemens is disturbed. Clothes would be better, he says. After all, no one on Fiorina has seen a woman for years. 'For that matter, neither have I,' he adds, his face hidden from her, by searching in a closet for things she can wear.

6

As they seek out the ship, Clemens tells Ripley (and us) something about this odd prison colony – built to house a thousand, but now with only twenty-five inmates. This accounts for the daunting scale, and the quality of loneliness. What do they make there? Lead sheets for toxic waste containers – with that, at least, this odd nineteenth-century future hooks back into our own times, for we are more than ever confounded about the adequate wrapping up and disposal of our own detritus. In the talk, Clemens addresses her as Lieutenant Ripley, and she wonders how he knows her name. It's stencilled in the back of your shorts, he says.

They reach the shuttle, and Ripley clambers in to investigate. He tells her the bodies are in the colony morgue, pending the investigation team. He describes how the deaths occurred: Hicks impaled, and the little girl drowned. Ripley weeps, and her lowered head sees the staining on the side of one coffin where acid has fallen.

Could those deaths have been accidental? Or are they the sport of the alien? In which case, evidently, it decided to let Ripley live.

'I have to see her in the morgue,' she says.

We cut to a room somewhere in the complex. One of the prisoners has found his dog – the brindle-coloured mongrel – and discovers that the animal is badly wounded in the head and jaws. There is blood, and the dog's coat is heavy and sticky with a kind of glue.

'What sort of animal would do that to a dog?' the prisoner asks himself.

Then we are in the morgue: it has a radiant blue-white light falling down across cabinets of drawers. Clemens pulls out one drawer. We see a white sheet drawn back and, too briefly for recognition, the face of Newt – in fact, the new actress for the part is Danielle Edmond. Ripley asks if she can have a moment alone with the corpse. Clemens and a morgue attendant back away.

Ripley looks at Newt. A big close-up shows us the child's eye open, the lashes still and curled. It is like looking at a doll's eye and reminds us of how Casey's eyes fluttered in the water in *Aliens*. Ripley closes the eyes. She feels the corpse's throat, its chest, and looks inside the mouth.

Clemens is puzzled, but much more so when Ripley says there will have to be an autopsy. I have to see inside her, she says. And she suggests that there could be a risk of cholera. There hasn't been a case of that for two hundred years, says Clemens.

'Please,' says Ripley.

We cut to the shining steel of an autopsy table, with a curl of clear fluid round the drain. There is the same blue light. We see the tools, the scalpels of autopsy. Clemens makes the gesture of an incision, and blood copies that loop of water. There are sounds of something in the body as he works, but we see just the faces of Clemens and Ripley. There is a splash of blood on his tunic. 'Everything's in place,' he murmurs, looking down.

'Chest?' she suggests.

He is startled. But he takes a saw. 'Careful,' she says – that makes him wonder – and he pierces the girl's thin ribs. He peels back the skin, and finds lungs, flooded with fluid. She did drown.

'Now,' he tells her quietly and not unkindly, 'since I'm not a complete idiot' (that is a very English remark, so full of native ambiguities), 'would you like to tell me what we're really looking for?'

She cannot answer. For Andrews and his assistant Aaron appear, descending a rusty spiral staircase. At such odds with the steely sheen of the autopsy table? Clemens introduces Ripley, and says she's feeling better. But Andrews is huffy. He has heard that Ripley has been out and about, and he wants to know why this autopsy was done without his permission. Clemens says there was some chance of infection. Ripley says there will have to be a cremation of the bodies – she hardly knows how to ask for anything now. Andrews is horrified, but the word 'cholera' does alarm him, and so he agrees to let Clemens handle it. But he must make himself clear to Ripley. His charges are all 'double Y chromeys' – 'all scum', murderers, rapists and so on. They may have taken up religion, but they're still what they were. And he wants no ripples in the water. She must be discreet.

7

The autopsy is selective. After all, the demon might have easily inserted itself inside Hicks – wounded, perhaps, but as good as the Marines had to offer. Ripley does not seem to consider that. Instead, she takes it for granted that the beast would have sought a female to play 'mother' – no matter that all this breed are, so to speak, the seed of Kane. The dread at the autopsy, and the spontaneous warning to Clemens (a mercifully inclined man), 'Careful', is founded in the anxiety that an alien is rooted in Newt. (We do not face the question as to whether a dead host could sustain life in the monster.) And if it is not in Newt then there's only one other place it can be. Of course, *Alien³* the would-be self-sufficient entertainment, has a serious problem here, for if Ripley is pregnant then that ought to come as a surprise. But it cannot, and so this film needs to turn into some sort of ritual in which the process of gestation is fulfilled (or not) with a concomitant spiritual discovery.

Further, deprived of her 'family' (as established in *Aliens*), what really does Ripley have to live for once she suspects that she is carrying a great demon – even a Queen's Queen? Did she not know the logic of 'kill me' in that fearsome dream she had at the outset of *Aliens*? Hasn't she been made more resolute by the action of that film, and more certain of the peril that these aliens portend? Does she think twice about destroying herself? Or – if she is to be torn – wouldn't that have to be because of some bizarre, yet credible, twist in her sense of motherhood?

I am beginning to depart from the set text of these films. But it has to be, because around this point the films become less than good enough.

8

We see the vents from the plant's great furnace, with an orange glow coming up from them. A few men are working. All the others are apparently assembled by Andrews. He had said that Clemens was to arrange the cremation, but this feels like his pompy show. With everyone gathered, he puts on his spectacles to read.

We see the dog pacing in its room. But what is it waiting for?

Andrews begins, 'We commit this child and this man to your keeping, O Lord . . .'

There are dissolved close-ups of all the men, and Ripley, watching. 'They have been released from all darkness and pain,' Andrews intones. But the dog is still pacing.

'The child and the man have gone beyond our world. They are forever eternal and everlasting . . .'

We see the shadow of the dog on the wall of its room, barking, barking, at what? Its fate? Its shadow? Its chance of eternity?

'Ashes to ashes,' says Andrews – he could be Wackford Squeers, burying a waif – 'dust to dust.' The second 'dust' rises in self-satisfaction.

But then, as if to erase the clerical rhetoric of one service, Dillon strides forward. The dog now is writhing and howling, unable to escape its own inner pain.

'Why are the innocent punished?' asks Dillon. This could be the dog's helpless protest. 'Why the sacrifice? Why the pain?' The dog drops on the ground, as if dead, or defeated by its ordeal.

We see a tear slide down Ripley's face, as Dillon goes on, about the child, 'She won't have the hardship of those left behind.'

Then we see two corpses, wrapped in white, one large, one small, dropping down into the vat of molten lead. There is a view from above of the falling shreds, and the brightness of the furnace – orange at its edges, then yellow, then nothing but white at the core. Ripley's face, her eyes at least, are within the suspended, melting dissolve of the shot.

There is something inside the dog, something aching to get free. A drop of blood slides down from Ripley's left nostril, which Clemens notices.

There is an explosion of blood and guts in the dog's room.

'There's always a new life, a new beginning,' promises Dillon.

And we see the newborn alien on the floor, breaking out of its protective membrane so that by the time Dillon and the others chant 'Amen!' the monster's two heads try to utter the word, too, the inner jaws stretching out with something that must be liberty.

We see the whole beast, staggering on its new legs, like Bambi. There is something of a malign innocence abroad again.

9

It's a very powerful scene – there's no denying that – even if movie connoisseurs can hardly miss the resemblance to *The Godfather*, and its ironic (?) mingling of slaughter and baptism standing for the Corleone ideology. But the overlap of liturgy and birthing is more intricate here, less self-satisfied, and more disturbing. The moment when the alien's ghastly head mouths 'Amen!' is not just a nudging, half-cynical, half-gleeful 'effect'. It's an arresting collision of the familiar and the uncomfortable, and a moment at which, no matter how ruefully or with what foreboding, we do recognise some elemental marvel in the alien. But what are we to make of Dillon's words? Is he just an idiot believer whose thought of new life is being cruelly mocked by the cross-cutting – or is there at least a chance that his faith, his tolerance, may admit a mystery greater than anything held in the frantic combat of *Aliens*? Where are we supposed to stand in the argument, if it amounts to that? Or are we just being set up for more chase-and-battle? Is the air of spirituality as empty as Andrews's cant, or does it portend something more searching? The only answers will depend on where *Alien³* goes – and they are not very fruitful. But here is a moment when the series came to the threshold of new developments – as when in the early 1930s Universal stumbled into seeing that Karloff and Elsa Lanchester together on screen could take *Bride of Frankenstein* further than the company had ever thought of going.

After all, if every one of these monsters wants no more than the chance to destroy all life – if they are that extreme a negative – then they do become tedious. The aliens need some greater cause or motivation – and it is alluded to in the notion that even an alien can stagger and shiver when it meets air and life.

10

Ripley washes her hands in a basin, and then reaches up to wipe steam from the mirror above her. This reveals a Ripley who has had her hair cut down to a stubble of crew-cut. She looks at herself – as well she might.

It is surprising enough that we have not had the scene in which the hair is cut (did she cut it herself? Did Clemens perform the service?). Wouldn't it amount to an intrusion, a loss of personality or sexuality – even if years ago, in basic training, just like a *G.I. Jane*, Ripley was shaved?★ But it seems even odder that this rebel has let it happen. After all, she knows that lice are hardly the most relevant threat on this planet. And yet Ripley suddenly goes bald . . . and the show is deprived of Sigourney Weaver's hair (one more step in the march of wilful self-denial). Weaver was also co-producer, which makes the meekness of the character all the harder to accept.

We hear the men gossiping – about how troubles only began when Ripley arrived – as she takes a shower. Then, dressed in grey, she enters the prison dining-room (a rather sophisticated place in terms of decor – shouldn't it be a hovel?). The men watch her as she gets food for herself. One prisoner closes his eyes and crosses himself. She wonders where to sit, and then goes up to Dillon's table. She says she wants to thank him for what he said at the funeral.

But he tells her, 'You don't want to know me. I'm a murderer and a rapist of women.'

'I guess I must make you nervous,' says Ripley, quietly, in a way that pierces his bombastic self-advertisement.

She sits down at his table, and there's some rather empty chat about faith, tolerance and the untolerable. The scene goes nowhere really, even if it helps build a bond between Ripley and Dillon.

Then we cut to another part of the complex where Clemens is talking to Ripley – there is an unfortunate air of them being the two white people in the settlement, talking about the natives. Clemens tells her how the prisoners found religion – a sort of apocalyptic, millenarian, Christian fundamentalism – and then asked to be allowed to stay on when the Company wanted to close the

★In Ridley Scott's *G.I. Jane*, Demi Moore cuts her own hair in a set-piece of dedication and ambiguous self-enhancement.

facility. So they remained, with two minders, Andrews and Aaron – and a medical officer.

She wonders how he got that job.

But he ignores her question and asks her how she likes her new haircut.

He asks her again what it was she was looking for in Newt's corpse.

And she wonders if he's attracted to her.

In what way? he asks.

In that way, she says.

All of which is very odd. What is uppermost in this Ripley's mind – her likely predicament, or a little bit of flirt? Does she want to have sex to restore faith in her lost hair? And why should she not explain the facts and her fears to Clemens? He is decent. He is 'her sort of person' – worthy of her club. He is actually rather effete beside the men Ripley fought with. He is not very compelling – indeed, he is less interesting than Dillon. He is a half-hearted plot direction that will never be taken up; he is a diversion. But we are left to suppose they are going to have sex, a thing that has never concerned Ripley. As if to prove that, we are not going to see the sex, or get any hint of how one modest, tender bodily invasion might set off pangs of . . . envy or territorial dispute inside her.

We cut to a large tunnel, the walls of which are being cleaned by the prisoner Murphy (Chris Fairbank). Beside him, at the end of the tunnel, a large fan is working, making striations of light and shadow.

He finds the discarded skin of an alien on the ground, picks it up, and is drawn to a nearby hole from which the alien leaps out at him and so wounds him that he is sent tumbling into the fan, which reduces him to small cuts and a spray of red.

As if startled by that dream, Ripley wakes up in bed. She turns over and sees the bar coding stamped on the back of Clemens's neck. Isn't it romantic? He is awake, and he gets up. 'I really appreciate your affections,' he says – slipping into a Coward dressing gown almost – 'but I am aware that they deflected my questions.'

They spar with words, and she lets him know she's seen the bar code. That does deserve an explanation, he admits – yet, truly, it doesn't. But a buzzer sounds for Clemens. It's Aaron with news of Murphy's death. So Clemens goes off on his duty, leaving a darkly thoughtful Ripley in bed.

Clemens finds Andrews and Aaron in the tunnel. He also notices a piece of acid-corroded metal in the floor. Andrews demands to see Clemens in his office. Then we find Ripley searching for a computer. Clemens comes up on her, and she tells him she wants to find the wreckage of Bishop. He points her in the right direction and then goes off to his meeting with Andrews, where the superintendent reprimands him and says he's just had a message from Network – the first ever received on Fiorina – saying that Ripley must be taken care of.

In the open air, on a waste site, Ripley finds 'Bishop' – half his head, the neck, a shoulder and an arm. She is about to make off with him when she is surrounded by several sexually predatory prisoners. There is the start of a rape scene – nothing very clear – before Dillon arrives and beats the men. He tells Ripley to take off while he re-educates some of the brothers. She goes, but not before slugging one of the would-be rapists.

In another part of the complex, we see several men working by candlelight. But a draught blows out the candles, and two of the men are duly killed by the alien. These killings are not just monotonous now, they risk being pointless or merely serial.

But we cut to the infirmary, where Ripley puts the remains of Bishop down on a table. She attaches an electrode to his neck, and screws into his head to insert wires. His hands flutter, and he comes back to the best 'ON' position he can manage – he likes her new hairstyle (enough to argue that Bishop has more comedy in him than his designers suspected).

'Can you access the flight recorder?' she asks. No problem, he says, and she taps him in on a keyboard. He reports that there was a fire in the cryogenic department.

'Was anything moving?' she asks. 'Was there an alien on board?'

He answers yes. It was on the shuttle all the way with them.

Does the Company know?

'The Company knows everything.' (Does the Company know about this conversation? If so, what a moment to flash us across space to Company controls, watching the sentimental scene on television.)

Then Bishop asks her to disconnect him – as a kindness. For he knows he can never be top-of-the-line again. That seems odd, since he's gone from garbage heap to perfect performer with just a few turns of a screwdriver. But Ripley does as he asks. She owes him that much. So now she's without all her old pals.

11

Golic (Paul McGann) is carried back from the candlelight killings. 'No one can stop it,' he says of the creature he has seen – he calls it 'a dragon'. Andrews says that Golic is stark raving mad: it's more likely that he himself killed the other two men. But Ripley comes in and assures them that Golic is correct; Dillon adds that Golic has never lied to him. Andrews is furious at being opposed. He orders Ripley to his office.

There, he hears her tale and scorns it. But Ripley is bemused when Andrews admits to her that this maximum security prison has virtually no weapons – 'We're on the honour system.' 'Then we're fucked,' says Ripley in a matter-of-fact way. But Andrews responds by confining her to the infirmary. 'That's a good girl,' he says, as she departs.

We cut to Ripley, with Clemens, in the infirmary. Golic is in a bed, listening to them, his head still wreathed in blood. Ripley is coughing. She complains of the heat, a sore throat, and feeling sick to her stomach. Clemens offers her another of his special cocktails.

Out of the blue, Golic asks her if she's married, and he recollects in a half-delirious way that the girls used to like him – 'for a while'. Meanwhile, Clemens is steadily examining Ripley, feeling the glands in her neck. And Golic suddenly blurts out, 'You're going to die, too.'

'Are you?' Clemens asks her, more considerately. He tries to get at her truth again, but Ripley reacts by asking him his secret. So he tells her the 'long, sad story' about how as a very promising young doctor – albeit a morphine addict – he once did a 36-hour emergency room stint. Finished, got drunk – and was then called back. There was a big accident, with thirty casualties; eleven of them died because he prescribed the wrong dosage of pain-killer. He got seven years in prison and had his licence reduced. But he did get off the morphine. So, when the other prisoners stayed, he stayed, too. Who else would employ him?

'Do you still trust me?' he asks.

To which, she offers her arm for his needle.

But why in the world have we had to endure this rather *Separate Tables*-like story (Charles Dance would be ideal in Terence Rattigan material) when, as he injects her Clemens becomes the next victim of the dragon. The creature simply slips open a ceiling hatch, drops down, and hauls the medical officer away, leaving a cascade of blood and the memory of a good needle man. The preceding scene is not just violated, but mocked for its futility. And another line for Ripley's development – though pale and thin – is cut off.

Only one valuable or piercing moment lingers. For the creature drops down again, and comes up to Ripley, slumped against the wall. Not to devour or ravage her. But just to eyeball her and to let its cold, gluey snout nuzzle her. The gesture is taunting and nasty – how much more intriguing it would be with a hint of fondness or curiosity – but it does clearly say, 'Look, sweetheart, I don't kill *you*. We're too alike.'

There's a cut, and we have Andrews again, in the dining-room, in his role as 'Rumour Control', addressing the diminishing number of his flock. He describes the deaths in the tunnel and the conclusion that Golic was the killer. Then Ripley breaks in, having run from the infirmary, with 'It's here!' Get that woman back to the infirmary, Andrews roars, and at that very instant the alien comes down out of the ceiling again and efficiently shatters the pompous little superintendent. When you've got more characters than you know how to handle, off them as quickly as possible . . . or hope that not too many viewers recollect the icy narrative precision of the first two films.

12

Andrews and Clemens are hauled away, with the same bloody gusto, in a matter of moments – and neither is missed. For, despite Brian Glover's flourish and Charles Dance's skill with a line, they neither of them mean enough to Ripley. Clemens may make love to her – we have to take it on trust: the most carnal discovery in that act involves the bar coding on the back of his neck. In *Aliens*, Apone, Hicks, Hudson and Vasquez – even Gorman – mean so much more because they have things to do, cinematic moments that are emblematic of character. In contrast, the woeful rendering of Clemens's past is flabby and redundant: no other character in the series is given such a backstory, or needs it. Remember how little we know of Ripley. The one brief interlude with a revived Bishop is the best human interaction in the film so far, even if Dillon holds promise still. Why doesn't Ripley insist on keeping Bishop 'with' her? Why doesn't that Bishop, say, observe the alien's nuzzling of Ripley, and tell her, 'He seemed to know you, Ripley'?

13

Command now has slipped down as far as Aaron, a man known as

85 to the other prisoners, because of his IQ statistic they found once when they raided the personnel files. Many of the men do not trust him – they want Dillon to take charge. But he's not officer material, he says; he just takes care of his own. This loose talk is played out over recurring close-ups of a silent Ripley, for in the end there is no other possible commander, just as she is the true cause of the situation. Aaron confirms that there are no weapons. Ripley says she's never seen an alien like this one before, but in the past they've always been afraid of fire.

She asks if they can seal off an area? No chance. The video system doesn't work – nothing works. Another of the prisoners, Morse (Danny Webb), begins to rant at all they lack: video, climate control, rubbers, women, guns, ice cream even. Just shit! And he wants to shove Ripley's head through the wall.

But Ripley and Aaron work out a plan. There is a toxic waste disposal site in the complex, never used. Get something in there, and it can't get out. They'll burn the creature out of the tunnels and into the disposal site. There are drums of a flammable material and detonators. But the plan goes wrong when one man climbs a chimney to find the monster there ready to bite off his head. He drops a detonator and the tunnels are swept by fire. Some more of the prisoners die before the sprinkler system can control the inferno.

We see the search for bodies afterwards, with a hand-pulled cart – yet again, this moment from the future could be from the Dark Ages we trust we have escaped. Like people waiting for Godot now, they have no workable ideas. There is dissent and panic mixed together. Ripley seems unwell. She leans against the wall, breathing hard, clenching her hands. 'I have to use the neuro-scanner,' she says – it is not the best line in the series, and it does take away from the medieval, plague-ridden air of the shit-coloured tunnels.

Followed by Aaron, she goes to find the CAT-scan machines. There are several of them, in a row, and they work: this colony can't get its natural order straight. She takes off her outer clothes and slides into the prone position in the scanner. The glass lid is lowered. But Aaron is there to help her with the keyboard. He taps in the data – 'BIOFUNCTION' – and hits 'ENHANCER' when the first pictures are muddled. Still, it's hard to read the image of the inside of her body. She lies still, the blue of the picture reflected in the curved glass of the lid.

'Keep looking,' she tells him.

And then he sees . . . how do we describe it? A seal frolicking in her guts? An embryo rearing its ugly, yet its own, head? The caption reads 'FOREIGN TISSUE'. Aaron's silence is as palpable as his horror – he is only an 85, after all, a simple soul. 'You've got one inside of you,' he says.

'It's not possible,' she says – but hasn't she feared this for half the movie?

She wants to see it. He tries to put her off. But she tells him to freeze the frame. And there it is, the poised eyeless head, gazing back at its examiners.

Ripley's reaction is wan, bitter, unbelieving, sorrowful – too conventional, not enough. There needs to be a trace of intellectual wonder, as well as madness.

We see the scanner on the roof moving.

'It's up,' says Aaron.

'Tell them the whole place is safe now,' she says.

He is shocked: such a report would make rescuers go away; and he wants to be rescued. Aaron, it turns out, has a wife and son to go home to. He can't quite see why Ripley wants to keep the peril confined, that she doesn't trust the Company, so he refuses to give her the code.

She sighs. Maybe she'll go find the alien then – see how smart it is. She leaves the bewildered Aaron. But then his computer screen delivers a message. The Company must have picked up the CAT-scan pictures. A medivac team will be there in two hours. It is absolutely top priority that Ripley be quarantined until then.

14

We see a ship making towards a planet, and at the same time Ripley goes on her solitary search of the tunnels. She has a flashlight, and she has some trouble breathing. Under her breath, she asks where the alien is when she needs it. Her light scans old pipes and ducts – those shapes, from the outset, have seemed the genetic code to the alien. 'Don't be afraid,' she croons, 'I'm part of the family.'

She picks up a heavy iron bar, and sees a large pipe that could be a resting alien. 'You've been in my life so long,' she says, 'I can't remember anything else. Now, do something for me. It's easy. Just do what you do.' There is a destructive, sexual longing in her voice.

Ripley strikes at the pipe with her bar, but it is only a pipe, old and corroded. It crumbles, and bugs of some kind spill out of it.

She moves away, looks up, and there it is, her alien, in the rafters above her. It drops down . . . and the scene cuts away.

There's so much here that's fascinating – the Ripley whose life has been taken over by the alien, as if it were her parent or her child; the sickly need for help; the intimation of dead and abandoned cities being the spawning ground for some monstrous new life; and the meeting of kin. But *Alien³* doesn't know how to write a scene of the two of them together – a meeting at least, a quality of understanding as well as horror, something not so very far from the perilous rapport Sigourney Weaver had with gorillas in another film. Of course, gorillas are apes, human-like, touching, noble, and so forth. Yet gorillas are alien, too, and Ripley is losing her sense of herself. But this film doesn't know how to undertake that journey.

Ingenious commentary has argued that the Ripley of *Alien³* stands for a victim in the age of AIDS, or cancer, or any disease in which another life becomes rampant in the body. That's a worthwhile point. And one might add the strange example she offers at a time when

abortion controversies were very fierce. But there's something else
that ought to come to mind: that Ripley, the very lone wolf, has
become part of another kind of family – one that needs the alien
beast to be more fully revealed, or explained. For why does the
alien want Ripley as a mother figure? Is it out of hatred, or love,
or some mixture of the two? For the story to be pursued into this
third episode, or movement, something of that depth, that basement
metaphor, needs to be uncovered.

15

Ripley returns from her encounter with the alien to find Dillon
holding a red-headed axe. 'It won't kill me,' she says, and she tells
him that she is impregnated. It's a Queen, she says, an egg-layer,
capable of breeding thousands more. She tells Dillon that it must
have got inside her during hyper-sleep.

'I can't do what I should,' she tells Dillon, which is hardly in keeping
with the forceful claims for feminist authority that have been made for
the early films – and hardly credible in a world so hostile. Instead,
she wants Dillon to kill her. As if to persuade him, she says that she's
dead already – she couldn't survive the 'delivery'. She asks him if he's
up to it.

'You don't have to worry about me,' says Dillon. And there is
a shot of the two of them in the same cage. But his remark is
ill-considered bravado – and a sign of the film's indecision – for
though he lets her spread herself against the bars, her back to him,
and though he makes to swing the axe back, he only strikes the
bare bars with it.

'I don't like losing a fight,' he decides – and surely we knew the
movie could not end then and there. Still, we've been played with
again, as a story direction was offered and withdrawn. The fable-like
certainty of the two earlier pictures is missing – and it seems to convey
a lack of fibre or resolve in Ripley, which is an impossible way to play

her character. But Dillon is left with a roundabout explanation: if the alien won't now kill Ripley, then that could help them fight it.

So the action lurches on, though Ripley extracts a promise: that if they do waste the beast, then Dillon will take care of her. No problem, he says. But do we trust him? Charles S. Dutton gives Dillon a great declaratory strength, but the film doesn't actually believe in its murderers as hard men. They may look like serfs from a Dostoyevskian underground. But they're full of liberal qualms and tough-mouthed rhetoric in which the word 'fucking' prevails. That's a pity, if only because of the one moment when the creature is called 'mother-fucker', and the suggestiveness of the remark is lost in all the 'fuckings' we have had to hear.

16

There is a council of war in one of the inner halls of the complex. Dillon proposes a concerted effort to destroy the monster. Aaron wants to wait for the rescue mission, which is bound to have guns. But Ripley tells him they will be no defence. The Company doesn't mean to kill the creature. Once upon a time, it was the crew of the *Nostromo* that was expendable. Then it was the Marines on the *Sulaco*. 'What makes you think they'll care about a bunch of lifers who found God at the ass-end of space?'

The question sinks in. Aaron is evidently perplexed and disturbed by the dilemma – he's a Company man, but should he trust the Company?

The plan Dillon proposes is very simple: they will lure the alien into the mould and then drown it in hot lead. After all, this complex is built around the lead-works, and all tunnels lead to it. Someone asks who'll serve as bait to draw the beast in, and the moment of silence lets the answer speak for itself. You're all going to die, says Dillon, and the only question is how you check out. The music builds in this scene to a crescendo with his 'I ain't much for begging.'

The chase begins, with the crouched figures of men scuttling away from a first-person Steadicam shot – in other words, from the point of view of the alien – seemingly going at a headlong pace.

But then the view cuts away, to the signal dish on the surface of the planet, and a distant view of the medivac spacecraft coming in to land.

There is a view of David (Pete Postlethwaite) peering round the corner of a tunnel and calling softly, 'Kitty . . . kitty', that goes back directly to Harry Dean Stanton's Brett in *Alien* – but just because of the echo it can't avoid seeming a little too ironic, or camp, now. It's hard to believe that the film-makers are still as afraid of the monsters as we want to be. Yet maybe that is just another way of saying that we are ready for a more sophisticated attitude.

Another variation appears: those first-person pursuing shots go upside-down – because the alien has different points of view, or to avoid the risk of boredom? David is killed: he fancies he has the monster on the far side of one of the sliding doors, but as he peers through the window to examine it so it looms up behind him. The howls of dying men echo through the corridors.

The spacecraft has landed. We see men emerging, making their way through a blizzard of debris blown by the wind. We see at least one man wearing a loose plastic coat. They move forward purposefully.

The plan of the tunnels and the movement of the aliens are not clear, yet the plan seems to be working. Ripley gives the order to set the pistons in motion which will gradually close the mould.

We see the rescue party coming towards the complex. There are men in spacesuits and several who wear plastic coats that are billowing in the wind. Aaron is waiting just inside the complex to meet the party. The apparent leader of the party, an Oriental, asks where Lieutenant Ripley is. Is she still alive? Aaron tells them that she's in the lead-works with the beast.

We see a figure in the group of men, standing a little back. He is lit from behind, so that he appears in silhouette. And he is as romantic as a figure in the J. Peterman catalogue★ – bareheaded, in a scarf and a long coat, a duster, carrying a briefcase.

In the crisis in the tunnels, Ripley has to go to meet the creature to get it into proper position. She backs it off, though it uses its tails to lash at her. Then Dillon appears. He drags Ripley away, and takes over her role as sacrificial victim who will keep the alien in the mould. As Morse climbs up to the controls, Ripley tries to argue. She wants to stay and die. But Dillon tells her, 'It dies first – then you.' Still, he can hardly honour his promise to settle with her if he is himself dead.

But Dillon takes off his spectacles, and advances down the narrow passageway of the mould towards an alien already furious at the feeling of being trapped. So Ripley shouts to Morse to release the lead. Like coins or splatters of paint, the molten metal falls into the mould and smothers Dillon and the creature.

On the platform above, Morse cackles and prances like an urchin who has overcome a dragon. But then suddenly, with some immense, elemental effort, the alien launches itself out of the molten lead and begins to climb up to the platform. 'Hit the sprinklers!' Morse shouts to Ripley. For he knows that water is scalding. She pulls on the chains that work the system and a deadly rain falls down. The creature writhes and groans and then breaks apart.

★The J. Peterman catalogue – available in America for several years now – advertises exotic, romantic clothes in a language that feels derived from movie hype and promotion.

'Gotcha!' cries Morse.

17

But not every problem has been solved. Ripley scrambles to safety on the platform – she and Morse are, apparently, the only survivors, along with Aaron. She is doing badly, bowed over, having difficulty breathing. She takes off her jacket. And then the rescue party appears.

'Don't come any closer,' she tells them.

And suddenly she sees that Bishop is in the group. He is that romantic figure from the catalogue – easily the most human of the group. We see him in a big, warm, sensuous close-up – the most romantic shot in the movie, perhaps. And he sighs, 'Ripley, I'm here to help you.' Like an old lover come back. Indeed, it would have been flat-out brilliant if someone had had the wit here to let him call her 'Ellen'.

Ripley is not to be fooled. She imagines that the Company has simply had the time and the resources to make a new model of 'her' Bishop, yet subtly programmed to be that much more of a Company man. He asks if she knows who he is, and she tells him a 'droid. No, he says, I'm not that Bishop. I designed him. I'm very human – human enough to make his great work in his own image.

This is a luminous moment, enough to convince us that so many of the earlier meetings in the movie have been half-hearted or unnecessary. For now Ripley is face-to-face with the embodiment of her paranoia – the Company impulse that has used her, and everyone else, to obtain a specimen alien for . . . study, analysis, taming, training and exploitation, presumably, when Ripley has learned only that the aliens are defiant of all such schemes and seek nothing but destruction. Well, not quite nothing. They do require the perpetuation of their own species – they must have some sense of kingdom or empire.

But for nearly three movies Ripley has given up so much of her real life, not least tenderness, motherhood, intimacy. The alien has become her life. And now the seductive Bishop speaks to that deprivation. He wants to take the creature out of her and take her home. You can still have a life, he tells her. Children. And you'll know it's dead.

'What guarantee do I have?'

'You have to trust me. Please.' He is Satan tempting her.

'No.'

The conflict is telling, but imagine if, somehow, Ripley had kept the old, broken Bishop as her help and confidant, and imagine now a confrontation between machine and maker – even one in which the machine knows the question that will expose the human Bishop.

Ripley turns to Morse and asks for his help. Aaron, realising how wrong he has been, takes a swing at Bishop, and is immediately shot down and killed by one of the men. Ripley stands above the vat of lead – she looks ill, drawn and harrowed, like Falconetti in Carl Dreyer's *The Passion of Joan of Arc*.* She has her back to the lead.

Bishop is filled with dread now. 'You must let me have it,' he cries out. But Ripley just leans back and does a reverse dive into the lead. Bishop roars in anguish, and as she falls so her alien, her child, breaks through the wall of her chest, an impatient, questing head, looking for life and having just a second or so before hot lead makes him one again with Ripley.

18

The rescuers depart, taking Morse with them, the only man who might tell the story. He laughs and snarls, the perpetual miscreant. Then there is a strange reprise of Ripley's voice from the end of *Alien*. The last message she read into the log, identifying herself as the sole survivor of the *Nostromo*. Then a computer screen simply records that the colony on Fiorina has been shut down and terminated. All at the behest of the Company – Weyland-Yutani: it is named at last.

*Dreyer is among the favourite directors of Vincent Ward.

Interlude

In its first run in American theatres, *Alien³* took in $31.7 million
– this in a year when *Home Alone 2* (a Fox release) earned $102
million and *Batman Returns* $101 million. The film picked up more
money overseas, and from some quarters it had the most intelligent
reviews of any film in the series. In *Film Comment*, Kathleen Murphy
responded to the rising religious feeling; in *Sight and Sound*, Amy
Taubin spelled out the AIDS metaphor. It was as if intellectual
and feminist critics had suddenly caught up with the resonance of
metaphor in the myth. The third film made money for the studio,
but it was a disappointment. Many audiences found the community
of religious prisoners perplexing and unsympathetic. Nearly everyone
missed Newt and Hicks – and Ripley's hair. And a lot of people felt
the series was out of its mind to kill Ripley – not just because that
seemed to shut down any future, but because people liked her so
much. There was also a point of view that missed the thrill of *Aliens*
and the guns. Even James Cameron recalled that 'Sigourney was a
little worried about the stuff with guns. I said, "What are you gonna
do, talk the alien to death? I don't think so."'

He felt that *Alien³*, and its absence of guns, showed Weaver's
influence. Cameron recalled how, in preparing for *Aliens*, he and
Weaver went to a firing range to practise with weapons. She grinned
and said it was fun, but he felt that the guns went against her liberal
instincts. And Weaver would admit that she preferred a Ripley who
was unarmed – of course, that also implied not killing the aliens, but

being ready to . . . live with them? And it was clear that the actress had embraced her own character's death – maybe because she'd had enough, because the third film had been the most embattled, and because there was crass talk at Fox of mixing the *Alien* and the *Predator* franchises together.★ Weaver would say, 'They're crazy to develop this great thing over the years and now they're just going to shit all over it.' David Fincher was widely blamed for what happened to the third film, but Weaver was his defender. 'The reasons that movie didn't work weren't David's doing at all.' Fincher had inherited the confusions of others, and so it is notable that in setting up the fourth film Fox took a much stronger hand. *Alien Resurrection* is still a Brandywine production, and Gordon Carroll, David Giler and Walter Hill are credited as three of the producers – along with line producer Bill Badalato (who had been on *Top Gun* and *Broken Arrow*). But the fourth film came into being because of Fox's initiatives (notably the push of studio heads Tom Jacobson, Tom Rothman and Peter Chernin), and without the same degree of input or control from Giler and Hill.

Of course, Ripley's death was a problem (if you were preoccupied with thoughts of sequential human drama), but it might be an asset – if you were ready to give science its wildest head. Questioned just after the release of *Alien³*, David Giler had said, 'The idea that she dies at the end, and it's a trilogy and it's over, is silly. If everyone loves this movie, there will be a fourth one. It's science fiction – there are nine million ways to bring Ripley back, or to do other alien stories. You could bring it back to the planet of the aliens, never mind Earth.'

Or simply trust the endless, inane fertility of movie-making: in genres other than sci-fi, the dead have returned with pretty explanations of how they survived. Sherlock Holmes did it once.

★By then Fox had also licensed *Alien* for comic books, toys and other games. Fox Interactive now offers an *Alien Resurrection* video game. Of course, the toys were aimed at an age group (under ten) arguably too young to be seeing the movies. But the licensing business seldom observes that much care or control.

And in the development of scripts, it is not uncommon for characters to go through death and rebirth a few times before the whole thing is worked out. Indeed, story-telling was ahead of science in the whole phenomenon of resurrection. We had thought of people coming back long before the notion or prospect of cloning.

It fell to Jorge Saralegui, a young executive at Fox, to reactivate the series. Years before he got into the picture business he loved the earlier films and 'didn't want to let it die'. He worked out a story-line of his own in which Newt was the new heroine, a grown woman yet a clone of her old self. When she died, the Company preserved her and now she takes on Ripley's role against a new outbreak of aliens. All of this was made necessary by Sigourney Weaver's apparent reluctance to continue with the series. Indeed, Saralegui was thinking of an actress like Bridget Fonda for the new Newt.

Saralegui hired Joss Whedon, the writer of *Buffy the Vampire Slayer*, to go with the idea. He did a 34-page treatment that won Fox's approval – they liked Whedon even more when he took on *Speed* and earned a reputation for being a team player as he did on-set revisions for *Waterworld*. But Whedon's progress was then forestalled by news that Sigourney Weaver might be tempted back – of course, it was plain that her yielding would be part of a very lucrative package for her, and it was felt by some that the actress was playing a canny waiting game. Well into her forties now, Weaver didn't find rich material elsewhere, even if *Death and the Maiden* (for Roman Polanski) was one of her strongest dramatic opportunities. Nothing else had Ripley's charisma, or clout.

So Whedon and Saralegui dreamed up ways in which Ripley might be cloned and brought back as a viable character. A script emerged, and Weaver said, 'I was seduced by [it], which is really good, the best Ripley I've ever gotten to play.' Indeed, she could be very eloquent about the new Ripley: 'She's from this landscape of death; if you have already died, you have a very different outlook on survival. She's not intent on saving people. She's more of a nihilist.' She also got at least

$11 million, an executive producer's role, and veto power over the choice of director.

Equally, she was given Winona Ryder as 'back-up'. Ryder, only twenty-six, was the young lead from *Dracula*, *The Age of Innocence*, *Reality Bites* and *The Crucible*, and she was surely intended as some sort of box-office insurance. But her role had no roots and little necessity. It could not rival the epic proportion and the new status of Ripley.

At any event, *Alien Resurrection* has the simplest and the most accurate screenplay credit of the series – written by Joss Whedon – which is enough to persuade us that simplicity is no more reliable than turmoil.

Danny Boyle (who had done *Shallow Grave* and was making *Trainspotting*) was approached about directing. He had lengthy talks with Ms Weaver and signed on. But he seemed put off, not by her or the script, but by the prospect of having to work on so big a picture with so large a crew. *Shallow Grave* had a vision of its own, an hallucinatory or druggie quality, but it was the result of independent film-making, modest budgets and frequent improvisation. David Cronenberg also declined the job, because he felt he wouldn't be left to do his own thing. Offhand, it is hard to think of another director more capable of returning the series to masterpiece status. Stuart Baird was also considered.

You can understand the reluctance. Ridley Scott and James Cameron had defined the series, and made two memorable films. In trying not to repeat those, one might easily fall into something crazy or wrong-headed – that was the general estimate of *Alien³*. Yet the task was now monumental: Weaver was going to be paid more than *Alien* had cost in all. The studio was very anxious to regain the franchise, and the actress wore a producer's hat, too. In modern movie-making, the decisive moments are all too often hedged by contractual commitments, and by the need to do something rather than nothing. In America, it seemed that the actress had taken over the series – so it was likely that the director would come from somewhere else.

Saralegui and Winona Ryder (who was working hard to make the venture work) suggested and Weaver approved Jean-Pierre Jeunet, which was nothing if not bold. In collaboration with Marc Caro, Jeunet had made two striking feature films in France: *Delicatessen* and *The City of Lost Children*. The latter was about a child and a giant battling with a mad scientist. That, plus the pronounced look of the two films, was what interested the studio. But Caro and Jeunet had worked as a team, and Caro was not invited. It had been their method for Jeunet to handle the actors and the camera, and for Caro to look after design and decor. In fact, Caro did offer a few ideas on appearances for *Alien Resurrection*, but Jeunet had to direct on his own – and he had to work in Hollywood, for this is the only *Alien* film made in America, on the Fox lot, on Pico Boulevard.

Bill Badalato came on board as the line producer. The photography was put in the hands of Darius Khondji, who had shot the two Jeunet–Caro films as well as David Fincher's *Seven* and Bernardo Bertolucci's *Stealing Beauty* – two films so different in colour tone as to prove Khondji's virtuoso skills. Indeed, he is the best cameraman the series has had, and he gave *Alien Resurrection* an eerie, steely look which came from leaving a certain amount of unexposed silver in the negative. In addition, he saw Ripley as newborn, 'Someone who was not only coming back to life but generating it, as if she was an enlightened person. I tried to light her differently than the others, as if she were translucent, as if the light came through her.'

Tom Woodruff, Jr and Alec Gillis, and their company, Amalgamated Dynamics Inc., again handled the alien effects. Nigel Phelps – from *Judge Dredd* – did the production design. Bob Ringwood – from the *Batman* films – did the costumes. And Harvey Schneid, Jeunet's French editor, did the editing. John Frizzell wrote the music.

There were language difficulties throughout the production – an interpreter for Jeunet was credited – and some friction between star and director. One day, when she was getting sick, Weaver felt 'there was something Jean-Pierre didn't want to focus on and I just had a

The classic image of mother and child: Ripley and Newt.

Searching for trouble in *Aliens*. And Ripley, Aaron, Andrews and Clemens in *Alien 3*.

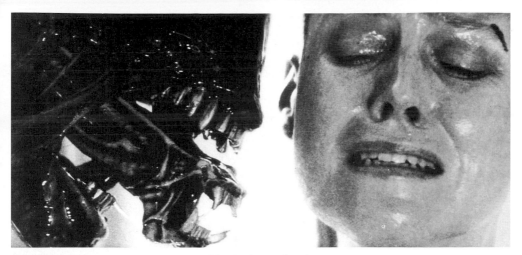

Tête-à-tête in *Alien 3*.

Ripley and Call in *Alien Resurrection*.

Mother and child - the new way.

sense of the rhythm the picture needed in order for the end to work. Jean-Pierre didn't agree . . . I didn't do anything big. I left the set for a minute, twice.'

Jeunet admits that there was a period of three days when their relationship, or trust, broke down. But they got over it, and Weaver took enormous pains to model her movements on those of the alien. By the time the film opened Weaver was working hard to promote it and vouching for the picture because she loved it. Intended originally for the summer of 1997, it was not ready in time, and so it was set to open on November 26th.

But the budget had gone to over $80 million, and at the same time Fox was dismayed by the failure of *Speed 2* and what seemed then like the approaching disaster, *Titanic*. Everyone at Fox was terribly tense, and Jeunet was doing all he could to get the picture without going over budget.

There were test screenings that got high scores. The studio was already thinking of *Alien 5* – which would be Aliens on Earth.

ALIEN RESURRECTION

1

The first thing to be said about *Alien Resurrection* is the saddest: it is that Part 4 does not feel like a part of the whole. Indeed, nothing is more helpful in composing the inner developments of the first three films – even in reconciling fans to that maverick, or betrayer, Part 3 – than the arrival of Part 4. There is an emotional arc and a consistent sense of tragedy in the first three films of the quartet: they carry a young officer through ordeal and apparent triumph all the way to self-sacrifice. As we comprehend the universe of the films at the close of *Alien³*, the first planet where aliens were found has been 'nuked', destroying them all. The one that got away at the end of *Aliens* has been blown apart by the scalding water at the close of *Alien³*. And the monster inside Ellen Ripley, so eager to get out and be born, was moments too late. It went into the fiery furnace where neither mother nor 'child' could survive. Bishop's last cry is one of loss – for Ripley maybe, but above all for the species that represented 'magnificence'. The story is done: Ripley has fought to the death, and won in the only way left to her.

2

We are on the *Auriga*★, an immense ship travelling through space. No hint is given of where it is going, or whether it has any journey to make. Perhaps in those future times existence itself is best conducted as an eternal travelling, or circling, in space. The *Auriga* is described as a medical research vessel; it may be that its delicate work is best done 'out there', away from contamination, and in a place where nothing that might go wrong could invade the Earth. If the Earth still exists or resembles the place we know. The ship has a crew of forty-two,

★The word means charioteer, but it seems to have no roots in Conrad.

with seven science officers. Those in charge of the science are Dr Wren (J. E. Freeman) and Gediman (Brad Dourif). The ship as a whole is under the command of General Perez (Dan Hedaya).

It is two hundred years after the rescue mission came to Fiorina just too late. We are in the medical laboratory, where we see in a large cylinder, as if sleeping or embryonic, the figure of a female – naked, hairless, its arms folded so as to cover its breasts. It is possible that the woman is Ripley, or some version of her. Yet it is younger than when we saw her last – it is another actress, Nicole Fellows. But then the woman seems to age (on a dissolve) and to become our Ripley, and we hear her voice repeating Newt's line from *Aliens*, about how her mother had once told her there were no monsters – yet there are.

We move to an operating theatre and someone very like Ripley is unconscious on the table. An incision is made in her chest, and then the doctors remove the early form of an alien monster from her chest cavity. The alien is slug-like, glossy with blood and mucous. It gives that urgent infant cry we have heard before, and then it is put in a clamp so that it cannot escape. Is there room for it to grow?

'What about her?' someone asks of Ripley. She has not perished in the procedure. 'How is the host?' the question goes. It seems she's strong, so the order is given to sew her back up. She is regarded as a 'meat by-product'. And shortly thereafter we find Ripley in a kind of arty solitary confinement, not so much a cell as an austere cylindrical pit where she lies at the bottom with guards pacing the translucent ceiling far above her. We see her, unconscious still, in a great sheet of some plastic or cellulose material. Then, as she slowly regains consciousness – or the artificial version of it – she uses her painted fingernails (they are purple – red and black) to break out of the membrane and feel her scar, as if, somehow, it is the secret to her existence. Without understanding, she sees a figure '8' tattooed on the inside of her fine arm.

3

Number 8, or Ripley, is quite evidently Sigourney Weaver, adjusted, as it were, for the age of forty-seven that Miss Weaver had reached by the time of the filming of *Alien Resurrection*. (She was actually forty-eight by the time it opened.)

This is a terrific forty-eight. There are lines at the corners of her eyes and mouth; and there is a kind of weary severity about her that has as much to do with Ms Weaver's experience as any ordeal of Ripley's. She does not look young, but there is little marked evidence of her wearing a lot of protective make-up, or being filmed in a charitable, soft-lens way. Rather, a kind of white light seems to radiate from her taut flesh; it is both 'attractive' in that nostalgic, sexual way we once knew, and yet suggestive of some kind of streamlined, guilt-free simulacrum – a 'perfect' artificial woman who may even have elected to look like forty-eight, because, after all, won't science of the twenty-second century know that that's where the several arcs of physical performance, acquired intelligence, emotional experience and pre-death acculturation actually coincide? By which I mean to say that given the business of cloning, might not Ripley, and especially Ms Weaver, have wondered, 'Couldn't I be twenty-two again?' But the sweet mixture of future science and actual cinematography has made her forty-eight look altogether neat, cool (very cool – you do feel that touching her could risk a chill) and very beguiling.

Plus if cloning means what we suppose it means, then this number 8 isn't going to have to get any older, is she? Did Ash and the original Bishop – the first one we saw, the artificial person – ever have to bother with the indignity of ageing?

Well, wait a minute. Sigourney Weaver is a co-producer on this picture, and she is earning somewhere in the region of $11 million for it, and we want her back – indeed, we concur with the eventual realisation at 20th Century-Fox (that name is awfully close to the archaic now) that the whole thing isn't worth trying without her.

And I don't think there's anyone in the audience let down by this lean, tall Ripley in a skin-tight brown leather outfit that lets her youthful arms swing clear and free, and where she has her own hair back again, even if it does seem to have been heavily, or ineptly, moussed – or is that just a little touch of the monster's gluey affection? So even if she isn't exactly or entirely her old self, we welcome her back – perhaps especially if she isn't, for that Ripley had grown sadder beyond her years, and I can't see too many objecting if this one has a little more of Ms Weaver's wit and a juiced-up respect for the fun side of life. She could even—

No, first things first. Why two hundred years? For that is what we will discover very shortly about the interval between films 3 and 4. It was poignant, early in *Aliens*, to learn that Ripley had been adrift for fifty-seven years – that surely added to her isolation and her being marooned out of her own time. But two hundred years is an altogether different abyss when, at the close of *Alien³*, Ripley had been so desperately on the cutting edge of 'progress'.

We will learn that the cloning work done to save the monster (and, as a side product, Ripley) relied on 'blood samples' from Fiorina. In other words, her brief stay in Clemens's medical laboratory was sufficient to provide the essential materials for cloning. But surely the real Bishop, the Bishop who led the rescue party in *Alien³*, would have known that. Indeed, if he didn't or couldn't command some magical, intervening scooping device – of the kind that so often altered the dynamic of cliff-hanging serial narratives – in other words, if he couldn't reach out and catch Ripley and her young one just before they splashed down in molten lead, or if he couldn't kill the furnace, suddenly reverse its temperature, freeze it, so that we could now have Ripley in the moment of suspended birth, like a statue within the great ingot or block of lead, then surely he went straight to the laboratory.

After all, as we saw in *Alien³*, the neurological scanner pictures that revealed 'it' inside Ripley were instantaneously transmitted back to the Company. So they surely knew of every other test or probe conducted by Clemens – they very likely observed the odd sexual communion he had with Ripley, and may have been crossing their fingers that the existing embryo wouldn't be made jealous or overly curious by other attentions.

Evil or not, dressed by J. Peterman or as severe as the life of the mind, Bishop seems like a genius at the end of *Alien³*. He is, at last, the clear manifestation of Company policy and overview. He is also an intensely arresting character. Is he not likely to surmise, in an instant, that blood samples waiting patiently in the laboratory – to say nothing of spittle, fallen hairs, scrapings of skin or even the dried frost of sexual juices on the sheets – will have a nice little code for the alien Queen, and for Ripley herself?

4

But two hundred years have passed! And to how little effect. It is all very well to pursue the ironic motif that as time advances so people's look and lifestyle seem to move backwards – give or take some innovations in weaponry. Two hundred years after *Alien³* life has hardly shifted: people are still watching inane TV shopping channels; a Scotch is made by hitting a slug of amber concentrate with a laser beam. The great flexing of science fiction is being nullified. Consider, two hundred years ago, in 1798, Nelson defeated the French at the Battle of the Nile (with iron cannon on wooden ships). There was no electricity, no telephone, no flight, no radio, no television, no computers, no birth control pills, no rock 'n' roll. Haven't we the right to expect that two hundred years from now – in 2198 – what with the natural acceleration in the pace of change, there will be drastic alterations in the way we live, even to the extent that the notion of 'life' may have to be redefined?

Yet *Alien Resurrection* has a kind of spacecraft that ran in the days of Ash. The *Auriga* probably serves the same arid cornbread that bored the crew of the *Nostromo*. So little has changed to give the notion of two hundred years its proper kick or rush!

But somehow 'they' have still waited that long to do the cloning that was on the tip of their tongues at the end of *Alien³*, and which, thanks to some Scottish sheep (and an American doctor named Seed), happened to be the talk of the town as *Alien Resurrection* was released. What happened to the ardour in Bishop's eyes, and his longing to 'have' the creature?

I ask that question because, despite the unusual intervals between the earlier *Alien* films, it was their trick and their cleverness to fit together as closely as possible. The flights that end films 1 and 2 are very tidily concluded, and explained, in films 2 and 3. This did wonders in terms of audience gratification and narrative coherence – it is even one of the beauties in the series, I think, that, after so long, the narrative personality comes back to the child in bed, after a telephone call, asks 'Where were we?', and picks up the tale so seamlessly.

Bishop at the end of *Alien³* is a credible representative of ultimate power in the world. He has come so fast to the rescue, with such resources, and he is not just an emblem of intelligence – he is the inventor of other 'life' forms. We could believe that he heads the Company or that he is appointed by its board to be chief scientific officer.

Whereas the authorities on the *Auriga* are of a very different kind. J. E. Freeman has it in him to portray a fearsome wickedness – who can forget his 'Dane' in the Coen Brothers' *Miller's Crossing* where he was not just the most astute antagonist Gabriel Byrne faced, but the most naturally cruel? But in *Alien Resurrection* his Dr Wren is not much more than nasty or creepy. He does not have Bishop's aura of wisdom or omniscience; he is edgy, easily frightened, small-minded – he could even be a rogue scientist who has somehow stolen the *Auriga* and the forgotten cloning materials, and gone off to do his naughty thing. That feeling is accentuated by having Brad Dourif play his assistant, Gediman. Dourif is an actor with a unique quality, but it has little to do with confidence, bold experience or treasuries of intelligence. He is a neurotic as an actor, and lo and behold, he is soon playing a childish game of 'Boo!' with the alien. As for Dan Hedaya's General Perez, the man is presented as a buffoon, a small-time conniver, and a very petty potentate. In the worlds of the *Alien* quartet, he should command not a major vehicle, let alone *the* vital research facility, but an old tugboat that carries crap to the dump.

These three characters belittle the *Auriga* and its work – it is as if the fleet that once had Conradian perspectives to live up to had been reduced to the level of comic books. That is a disastrous lapse in tone, for in the first three *Alien* films, and in the mind of Ripley, the fate of the world was being decided. And in *Alien Resurrection* we no longer feel compelled to take sides in that large struggle. That is all the greater a loss in that, ethically and metaphysically, very large questions are coming to a head in this film. But if the tone gets more facetious while the issues become graver, then the film as a whole seems sophomoric and opportunistic.

To take one example of that: in the trailer for the film there was a fine moment of conversation between Ripley and Johner (Ron Perlman), in which he came up to her in the first awareness of the perils in fighting aliens, because he'd been told that she'd done it before. What did you do? he asks her, and, with just a flicker of amusement in her eyes, Ripley says, 'I died.' In the trailer, in isolation, it seemed possible that that exchange was something like philosophy, an inquiry into profound differences between life and death even. But in the movie itself it is nothing but a cute one-liner – the cuteness of which, of course, had been given away in the trailer. And that, in miniature, is a model of the cynicism and apathy of so many modern movies.

5

Every imperative of story suggests that the cloning should have been carried out immediately after the end of *Alien³*. Thus the *Auriga* should be the ship that brought Bishop to Fiorina – he has said that it has surgical facilities. And Bishop should be in charge of it.

We will learn that the *Auriga* is part of an entity called United Systems Military which, because of 'United', gives some sense of being 'international'. (And the *Auriga* is under a 'General'.) The Company, we are told, folded up a long time ago. But what's the point in that for us, beyond the attempt to fill two hundred years? Since U.S.M. is, to all intents and purposes, the Company in a new guise, we might as well stay with the Company and with its best man – Bishop.

I will argue his case more fully soon. But for the moment let me just add this: that cloning has produced seven Ripleys – not quite accurately – before number 8. Very well. But where are 1 to 7 for the alien, then? How long has cloning been going on? as the song asks. And wouldn't it be nice to have just a little of the saturnine Bishop explaining the process to us and . . . well, getting a little involved with his work? I mean, isn't the Bishop at the end of *Alien³* the most challenging human mate Ripley has ever met? Remember the look in his eye when he said she might yet have children?

6

Once the situation on the *Auriga* has been outlined, with Ripley's serene warning – 'It's a Queen. She'll breed. You'll die.' – and Wren's feeble hopes for taming the creature, along comes the *Betty*. This is a kind of pirate ship, a small freighter with a crew of six – Elgyn (Michael Wincott), the rough-voiced captain; Hillard (Kim Flowers), his woman; Johner, a scar-faced hulk; Vriess (Dominique Pinon), a cripple in a wheelchair; Christie (Gary Dourdan), a dreadlocked black weapons man; and Call (Winona Ryder), a bright-faced young woman. There may have been thoughts in the preparation of *Alien Resurrection* that this crew might supply the gutsy texture of the Marines in *Aliens*. But it doesn't follow. The crew of the *Betty* are outward show without substance. They do comprise the soldiery in the film's running battle – in which only three of them will survive – but they never help us to forget that, by now, we have seen enough chase scenes and gun battles with the aliens. Indeed, it is a central failing in *Alien Resurrection* that it doesn't recognise just how familiar, and predictable, these monsters have become. In all the earlier films the policy of showing the creatures fleetingly, and in fragments only, kept their menace because we seldom saw them whole. But in *Resurrection*, the proud effects-makers have their work shown in full, in loving detail, too early, too often and with expected results. The aliens begin to be tedious (and dull!).

All the more reason, therefore, to do something that develops them or that poses novel and more sinister relationships between them and the humans. Moreover, such a direction is in sight – it has been there for two films, ever since Ripley's blackmailing threat made the Queen draw back in *Aliens* and her condition brought out a certain sardonic protectiveness in the bitch in *Alien³*.

Worse still, the crew of the *Betty* are not natural receptacles for our sympathy, for they have travelled to the *Auriga* with a delicate cargo – cryogenically preserved live bodies in which the alien eggs may germinate. Elgyn delivers his cargo and receives that measure of booty from another age – a suitcase full of lurid banknotes (a currency that hardly exists nowadays, as General Perez claims).

Their delivery done, some of the crew of the *Betty* adjourn to the *Auriga* gym, where they find Ripley at solitary basketball practice. She is no longer downcast or confused. Rather, she is an ideal specimen, so adept at ball control that she easily makes a fool of the clumsy Johner, keeping the ball out of his reach and then bouncing it at him with

great force so that it smashes into his groin. These manoeuvres are
a little lady-like; they don't really dazzle us or extend Weaver, who
took special training for the sequence. But there is one coup – when
Ripley throws a three-point shot over her shoulder, doesn't bother
to look, and hits nothing but net. There's a very satisfied look on
her face, and I'm happy to believe that it was shot for real (with
however many takes). But film isn't what it was. When Katharine
Hepburn sank the long putt in *Bringing Up Baby* (1938), one took
it for granted that the ball, the green, the putter, and the moment
were all that Howard Hawks had. But today, if Weaver couldn't get
the shot after hours of trying you know that technology could come
to her aid. We're not even sure now whether a movie star is walking,
talking or giving us the eye all on her own.

There's a scuffle between Ripley and the *Betty* boys in which she
gets a bloodied nose – do you remember the drop of blood that ran
from her nose during the funeral in *Alien³*? She wipes the blood
away with her hand, flicks it at the floor, and there's a nice little
sizzle and a modest erosion as her acidic content hits the metal.

7

Another problem appears. Since the days of Ash, and all through
the Bishop era, Company policy had been to preserve and study
the alien. Bishop, the inventor, even said there was a fortune to
be made from it, at the end of *Alien³*, and I don't think he was
proposing fairground shows. Still, it's easier to believe that the
scientific imagination is more drawn to the unalleviated hostility
of the creature, and its lethal efficiency, than to long-term notions
that its gluey excretion might make a wondrous coating for cooking
utensils, or even that a dilute version of its acid plasma could pep up
geriatric geniuses. Just what can the alien do for an advanced society,
beyond playing Grendel in its wishful dreams?

As if to illustrate that quandary, we now move to watching

Gediman in some special inner laboratory where he has the alien itself inside an unbreakable glass container. Is this the Queen so lately taken out of Ripley's body? I think it must be, though it does not look like the Queen as shown in earlier films (and later in *Resurrection*). If it's not the Queen, then does that mean that the *Auriga* had at least one other specimen?

Keep moving, and notice how Gediman has nothing to do but taunt the monster by staring at it, and pushing his own unlovely head close to the glass. The monster snaps at him, and then spits. Whereupon, Gediman hits a red button that submits the creature to a quick steam scalding. Must all science end in mere torture? And when the creature threatens attack again, the scientist's hand has only to hover over the button and the beast backs off. 'A fast learner!' says Gediman. If only we could say as much for him.

Meanwhile, Call insinuates herself into Ripley's cell. She takes out her knife and seems about to strike when she sees the tidily sewn-up wound in Ripley's chest. Number 8 awakes (as if because of the presence of another) and asks Call if she is searching for 'my baby'. And then to prove her own inhuman status, Ripley takes Call's knife and jabs it through her own hand – is that intended to represent a crucifixion? Should we wonder whether the blade may dissolve on contact with her blood?

Call is apparently the agent of some resistance-like group, aware that Ripley was host for the alien, and thus sent to kill them both. Don't ask where or what that resistance group is. Or how Call knew. But Ripley laughs at the 'humane' effort and says, don't you realise, Ellen Ripley died two hundred years ago. Who am I then? she asks – a thing? A construct?

8

It's a fair question, and one an actress needs to answer – if not a character. 'In this new one,' said Sigourney Weaver in an interview, referring to the fourth film, 'she's unleashed, totally unpredictable. Even *she* doesn't know what she's going to do . . . I felt Ripley should come back almost like a vampire. Her skin should be radiantly fresh, an element that makes her sexual and incredibly lustrous. She's almost too good to be true, and you don't know where she's getting it from. I wanted her to look "new and improved", strong, a little bit like a "creature". I didn't want to carry a gun. I mean, once you've died, it's not a big deal to die again. I thought it was important for her not to need all that paraphernalia.'

There speaks a co-producer, as well as an actress; and an actress with Sigourney Weaver's intelligence. And the answer she gives is a way of defining the dark, laconic fatalism of Number 8, as well as the rather icy, or acidic, glow she gives off. The woman on the basketball court is uncommonly strong (like a woman made of steel), though her strength is not really exploited in the combat scenes later. She does look lustrous, and sexually rapacious, even – for there is an unhindered appetite about this Ripley. (But she has no one upon whom she can visit those urges.) But can the *Alien* stories work properly if Ripley 'doesn't know what she is going to do'? Or isn't there the risk that a truly amoral or insouciant Ripley gives up the moral identity of the films? How much does Ripley remember? Does she think of herself as '8' or as 'Ellen' – a name she uses? Does memory come back slowly, and with it the burden of responsibility; or is she truly 'unleashed', unattached to her own past or any need to save the human race? If the latter is true, then she is a predator – and maybe very funny, very entertaining – but what is the film about? And why make it?

On the other hand, there is something very dramatic, or touching, in the prospect of a new, wild, unleashed force who gradually comes back to herself and her tragic role in the story.

9

Suppose, instead of what we have, that we are on a vast, streamlined spaceship – something with design pretensions, with pizazz, with decor by Travis Banton or Ferdinando Scarfiotti, not one of those clunky, turreted dinosaurs with the air of an old blacking factory. As this ship (let's call it the *Narcissus*) surges through space, we are in a magnificent enormous room – somewhere between a boudoir and a salon – with high windows, as large as movie screens, through which we can see the aqua infinity of space, the firefly stars, and trailing away behind the ship the sparkle of its own wake. There is a canopied bed in the room, with drapes and bedclothes made of silk and gauze. And there in the bed, asleep like Sleeping Beauty, is Ripley, the figure '8' clear in her exposed armpit. She is naked on the ivory sheets, her dark, matted hair spread out like the Medusa's head on her pillow. There is a fresh-sewn scar between her breasts, straight as a rule.

She is being observed by a nurse, and by the original Bishop, the great inventor, the master of the ship. (He is wearing a doctor's costume, but a doctor out of Africa, as it were.)

'She'll sleep,' the nurse says. 'But she'll recover. She's very strong.'

'That's why the Queen chose her,' murmurs Bishop.

We see his eyes gazing at her, and it is apparent that Bishop is more moved than he ever anticipated, that he is stirred by this Ripley he has reclaimed from death. He is seeing anew.

'And when she awakes,' the nurse continues – she is holding an empty syringe to suggest the use of drugs – 'she'll remember nothing.'

'Can we be sure?' says Bishop.

'The cloning was merely physiological. There's no trace of memory, of her past, her personality.'

'Unless she catches sight of herself.'

'We have removed all mirrors from the chamber, sir,' the nurse assures him.

10

There are other things to be noted in Ripley's meeting with Call in *Alien Resurrection*. First of all, Ripley seems attracted to the young girl, in ways she does not quite comprehend. She strokes her face, threatens her with great force, and yet seems to want to inhale her. Ms Weaver has said that she relished the rather 'kinky' elements in the new Ripley, the novelty of her appetites. For the new Ripley has hints of amused amorality – of being ready to take or eat anyone. Even of being a little bit of a monster. That power possesses some inexplicable instinct that seems to know when the creature, the alien, is moving or agitated. One of the most impressive things in Weaver's acting in *Alien Resurrection* is this alertness to psychic atmosphere, or rather the animalistic capacity to feel or register things outside the conventional human range.

Call leaves Ripley's cell, but is immediately apprehended by Dr Wren, who recognises her as a 'terrorist' on a mission to destroy his charges. This leads to a sudden confrontation between Wren and his soldiers and the crew of the *Betty*. There is a shoot-out, and the crew members triumph because of their extra 'piratical' skills – Christie kills one of the soldiers by bouncing a bullet off the ceiling so that the ricochet pierces the stooge's helmet. Dr Wren and another soldier, Distephano (Raymond Cruz), are captured by the *Betty*'s crew.

Gediman sees this 'emergency' on a television screen, but he is too distracted to respond. For three of the aliens, seeming to sense a time of general upheaval, develop their own insurrection. Two of them turn on a third. They tear at it and puncture its body so that a great rush of acid melts away the floor of their cell. They escape, leaving only the corpse of the dead alien in the cell. Gediman goes in, to examine the damage, looks over into the abyss and is gripped by the great claw of an alien and dragged into the hole. When another soldier enters the cell, a cunning alien appears at the controls and hits the steam button so that the man is scalded to death.

In her cell, Ripley feels this violent alteration in the order of things, and smiles with anticipation.

There is chaos on the ship. Aliens are free. General Perez is awoken. He gives orders to abandon the *Auriga*. But in the turmoil most of his soldiers are killed. Perez himself dies, pierced in the back of the head by an alien and reaching back to grab a handful of his own scrambled brains. In a brief frenzy of action, the *Auriga* is shaken by two revolutions and left as a perilous place from which the crew of the *Betty*, with Wren, Distephano and Ripley, must try to escape. Wren tells them there are twelve aliens, and Ripley promises that there will soon be many more.

11

Back to the *Narcissus* where, more than ever, we feel as if we are in the best stateroom of a luxury liner cruising for ever. There is some moody music in the background – it might as well be Sinatra doing 'I've Got You Under My Skin' – and the windows give us one more panorama of space in which suns seem to be rising. There is a great wash of cream, amber and raspberry in the light. Ripley, in a long gold-coloured skirt, but naked above the waist, is sitting back in a chair eating figs. These might be her first, and they are perfect figs. So, much as she relishes them, she is a little inexpert yet, enough that the ripeness runs down her chin and falls on the healed scar between her breasts. She dabs up that stray juice and, in the process, feels the scar. She draws a finger along its line, and on her face we see feelings of pleasure and loss unaccountably mixed together.

We realise that Bishop has come into the room and is watching her. He seems more than usually wind-blown – his long hair is untidy, though that only makes him more handsome – and he wears the sort of clothes that might be expected of an Existentialist adventurer in the Peterman catalogue. Ripley notices him.

'What are these?' she asks, indicating the figs. There is something oddly yet charmingly halting in her speech. She is, evidently, a mature or grown woman; yet her command of words is like that of a child who is only beginning to master the process.

'Figs,' says Bishop, and she repeats the word a few times to possess it.

'Figs are good,' she tells him, earnestly, but then she starts to giggle, as if reminded of other good things.

'You shall have them whenever you wish,' he says.

'We will do other good things?' And there is a smile on her face, like that of a child who has only just learned the power of pleasure.

'Would you like that?' he wonders.

She does not answer, but the way she gets out of her chair and crawls across the floor towards him is answer enough. Kneeling at his feet, she places his hands on her breasts.

'Here we go again,' says a voice – it is the nurse, and she is outside the room, with a laboratory technician. They are watching Bishop and Ripley, making love, on a television monitor.

'My,' says the technician, 'she's more aroused than ever.'

'He made a few adjustments in her overnight,' says the nurse.

'Every man should have one like her.'

'Or vice versa,' says the nurse.

'Oh! Look at that,' says the technician.

We cut into a scene of intense sexual interaction in which Bishop (still clothed) is somehow the detached surveyor of the great landscape that is Ripley, who is lost in a rapture so great that she begins to see the child's delight and the grown woman merging. She makes uncommon noises in her love-making, not just the sighs and groans appropriate to this sort of 18 certificate scene, but harsher noises, more guttural, fiercer and less human. In turn, those noises dissolve aurally to the attentive roars and admiring hisses of a group of aliens. Faraway in their quarters, but watching the same scene on their video display unit (everyone has TV). There are resemblances between the humps and curves of the human bodies and the glossy black forms of the aliens. We are reminded yet again of how sensually they are made.

12

As the crew of the *Betty* attempt to make an escape, Elgyn their leader is distracted by the sight of two weapons dropped in a side passage – a rifle and a pistol, granted that these are modestly futuristic extensions of those things. He goes to investigate, and he finds that the pistol is covered in a kind of gum. As he stands on the grating, claws reach through it and pull the metal down so that Elgyn falls. As he hangs there, the alien strikes at him and kills him. Elgyn's crew are devastated when they find the ruin of their leader. But they are chased from his body by another beast, which pauses and then goes back to sniff at the open wound in Elgyn's chest. As its head lowers, its mouth agape, a gun is thrust through the wound from below. It fires, and blows off the alien's head. And Ripley emerges from below, rifle in hand.

Without its leader, the group risks disintegration. Then Ripley feels that the ship is moving, and Wren admits that in any emergency it will return to home base – which in this case is Earth. Johner groans: 'Earth, man, what a shithole.' It seems like a place no one now wants to revisit. But the *Auriga* will make its landfall there in only three hours, and Call, for one, fears the dangers of aliens being unleashed on 'home ground'. There is talk of blowing up the ship, and Call argues that Ripley cannot be trusted. After all, she's one of them. But the group overrules her, and the sardonic Ripley gives Call a sympathetic grin. And so they begin to make their way back to the *Betty* – if they can.

Along one corridor Ripley is stopped in her tracks by a door that bears the sign '1 to 7'. The others tell her to hurry along, but she cannot resist the chance for something that explains the '8' on her arm. Indeed, as in a fairy-tale, no assigned princess or beauty can ignore the process that offers an answer to her own riddle. To fulfil her own story is the highest purpose of such a life. However, that does not necessarily guarantee that the anecdote along the way will erase all sense of mystery. For, in turn, the deepest function of mystery is to resist the explicatory thrust of story.

The room is a chamber of horrors, a set-piece, and on the surface at any rate something to make us 'think'. For the brightly lit laboratory contains six large glass cylinders in which there are specimens – the first attempts by Dr Wren and company to produce a Ripley (Number 8). They are 'hideous' in a spectacular, schoolboyish way (indeed, they are the basis for the disturbing close-up studies of deformity – with just one bright, correct eye – that go beneath the credits). There are figures with tails; mouths on the side of the head; grotesque humps and excrescences and, in general, every horrid 'error' in anatomy that one might find on *The Island of Dr Moreau* (I wondered if some of the props hadn't been ordered in from that grisly and atrocious film of a couple of years before).

In fact, I recall *The Island of Dr Moreau*'s creatures as being more revolting. The wild or aberrant forms in *Alien Resurrection* are rather cheerfully grotesque, and they cannot help but make us marvel at the sudden 'getting it right' that made Ripley out of Number 8. The figures in the cylinders are dead (I think); they are numb, dumb, hellish yet crude. Whereas the new Ripley is attractive, smart, strong, uncannily intuitive and given to a nice kind of deadpan irony. She is a little like the 'bride' in *Bride of Frankenstein* crossed with Lauren Bacall in *To Have and Have Not*. And if the purpose of this strange scene is to make a case against cloning (in the solid way, for instance, that President Bill Clinton is opposed to it), then it might have pondered more fully the dynamic change between these seven wrecks and Ripley. Getting to her in eight tries doesn't seem so far-fetched a gamble, especially if the medical staff had the sense to incinerate its failures (in the manner of any abortion clinic).

Furthermore, we wouldn't be at the movie if we hadn't wanted Ripley back: our need for life is a good deal more intricate or sophisticated than this trundling morality. One to 6, I think, could have been abandoned, if we kept 7, for that is the piercing memory. Seven is alive, albeit tortured and desperate. Seven lies on an operating table still. There are tubes in her abdomen. She has terrible scars, and although she is not dramatically malformed the actress playing the part conveys an unbearable pain and humiliation. The actress is Sigourney Weaver, and it is her imploring gaze that arrests Ripley. It is her mouth that whispers 'Kill me' – the very plea that Ripley made in her dream in *Aliens*. Far more than the specimens, this 7 conveys authentic horror – think what it could have done on its own, leaving us to imagine 1 to 6.

So Ripley takes the flame-thrower Call hands her. She is in tears, yet she pours liquid fire over all the cylinders and – after a nod of assent from 7 – on her own gruesomely pregnant image. The room is turned into a chamber of fire.

13

On the *Narcissus*, that five-star spaceship, a kind of paradise obtains. Ripley, by virtue of her fresh blood, her old repressed nature (the lovely woman who never got any love) and Bishop's fine hand on her behavioural controls, has become a kind of space nymph, a sexual performer capable of breaking her own records at every outing. So much so that she begins to exhaust even the ideally poised man-of-the-world Bishop. (The narrative potential of a Frankenstein figure who creates a perfect fantasy woman, but who is then gradually killed by her insatiable needs, is not without promise or humour.) And so we come to a scene in the great bedroom of the *Narcissus* where Bishop has been reduced to a profound sleep (not far from coma – Lance Henriksen's sunken eyes have only so far left to sink), while Ripley is still awake.

Something like boredom or disaffection overtakes her, some inner disquiet that not even multiple orgasms have muffled. She stirs from the great bed and notices the wan reflection of her body in the large black glass of the observation window. This is her first mirror. She stands, turns, models in a diffident and childlike way, and then appreciates her nakedness. She is disconcerted enough to draw a sheet from the bed and wrap herself in it. Then she goes up to the glass – to the prospect of space and its passing night – and sees, for the first time, the image of her own face.

She does not know how to look at herself. Is it a stranger – from out there? Can it be herself? She makes elementary tests, to see if the image matches what she does. And then she mimics the ecstasy of orgasm and is perplexed and troubled by the abandon in herself. Something like memory or identity begins to stir. She goes back to the bed and looks down at the sleeping Bishop. The bedclothes are so gathered at his throat, his head is so turned, and his manner is so wasted that she half-glimpses a shot of the shattered, discarded head of Bishop the android, the head she reactivated at the dump in *Alien³*. Without understanding, her mouth asks, 'Bishop?', and the real Bishop, her lover, awakens, a look of alarm on his face.

14

On the *Auriga*, still, as the would-be escapees search for a way off the ship, they come to an incubation room where the frozen bodies that the *Betty* traded to Perez were set up, clamped in place, in front of the alien eggs so that the claw and the arm could come out of the egg, seize the human face, slide into the body, wait and grow larger, and then burst free. The humans are dead, of course; every one of them has a gaping application of red jam on its chest. But one man is not dead or hanging in place: a wizened wreck named Purvis (Leland Orser) is slumped on the floor. He's alive still, though not feeling well.

Ripley comes up to him, for all the world like a hungry shark sniffing at bait. She puts her head close to him. She smells him and seems to measure the varieties of his life. 'Leave him,' she says curtly. 'He's got one inside him.'

Purvis is so horrified at her suggestion, he tries not to understand it. He pleads his case, though the others are ready to eliminate him and his happy event on the spot. 'Who are you?' he asks Ripley, and she answers with macabre satisfaction, 'I'm the monster's mother.'

She says that line so well, with such dark humour, and darker insight. But it's a perilous remark if the film's tone and context can't sustain it. It runs such a risk of being jokey, a wicked, ball-breaking one-liner, when it needs to be a simple admission of a very difficult nature. This needs to be what the film is about, for we've gone too far to be merely terrified by the new breed. We want to know them better; we want to understand the family.

15

'Where do I come from?' Ripley asks Bishop. She is not so fond now. 'What am I?'

'You're a woman,' he says. 'A prize among women.'

'What do women do?'

Bishop smiles, in a world-weary way: 'Whatever they want to do?'

Now she roars at him – there should be flashing teeth and more force in the sound than is entirely human: 'But what do they *do*?'

'Do?' Bishop is rattled by the signs of the beast in her. 'Women carry children to birth. That is the tradition.'

'Children?'

'So the human race can go on.'

'What are children?'

'They are the very young, the very small ones.'

'Is this children?' Whereupon Ripley withdraws one of her hands that had been inside the sheet she wears. The fingers and the palm itself are covered in blood. This may be the first menstrual blood

that the new Ripley, Number 8, has passed. Bishop is transfixed by
the sight, for he knows the blood is acid.

'How do I have children?' she asks him. 'Is it in the loving
we do?'

Bishop is very quiet now; nearly all the manner of authority is
stripped away. He cannot keep up with the instincts in the creature
he has made.

'It can be that way,' he says.

'We do it now,' she tells him.

'That's not possible,' he says, his voice no more than a whisper,
and this short scene ends on her very resolute gaze and the teeth of
her smile as she smears her own blood on her face like war-paint.

16

The people on the *Auriga* reach the cooling tower. And they descend.
But the lower level of the ship is flooded, and so they face a 90-foot
swim, through the kitchen, on the way to safety, that is entirely under
water. Christie, by now, has Vriess strapped to his back. Hillard – as if
a poor swimmer, or prone to claustrophobia – dreads the underwater
swim. But they all set out, making their way through a large kitchen
where spilled crockery lies on the floor like sea-shells. We see the
swimmers and the bone-white underwater look of their flesh. We see
the bubbles of air slip from their nostrils. Some are strong swimmers
(Ripley, of course), while others pad along with their hands on the
ground. (Weaver developed a swimming style – fish-like – to match
the monster in her.)

But why should a movie like this go under water if not to provide a
battleground new to the series? And so, soon enough, as the swimmers
look back they see the wicked fin-and-tail shapes of creatures pursuing
them. Johner shoots at them. We see the plug of bullet going slowly
through the water. One nimble alien dodges it, but it hits and
explodes another. There is an authentic panic and desperation as

one alien comes up on Hillard, bites at her legs and draws her away to drowning, or worse.

The others make it through the kitchen and look up at a cloak of heavy membrane that covers the water and keeps them from fresh air. They fight and shoot their way through it, only to discover that 'safety' is a resting area – a pool, as it were, surrounded by alien eggs. With the arrival of people, claws begin to stir from these eggs. One leaps out and grabs Ripley so that she is plunged back into the water, wrestling with it.

17

Bishop is dead. Come along now, don't act surprised or expect this scenario to spell out every last detail for you. There is only so much acid a Peterman genius can take – and yet no fitter way for a connoisseur cocksman to go. But Ripley finds keys in his pocket, and so she is able to leave the great room where all her life seems to have occurred.

She finds herself in a corridor. There is a door facing her, and one of the keys opens it. She goes into a room as large as her own, but impossibly overcrowded and untidy. Indeed, this room is the antithesis of design; it is the den of some great, neurotic accumulator. There are no windows. Just equipment, many shelves of books, stacks of paintings, statues, an office area, nearly smothered in papers. Though enough in the room bespeaks culture, knowledge and its pursuit, the disorder is akin to madness.

But on one table, with loose wires dangling from it, Ripley finds the head and shoulders of Bishop the artificial person. She is very moved by the materialisation of this thing she thought she had dreamed. She picks up the wires and pushes them into an available socket – the remains of Bishop quiver and tremble; his eyes open; a ghost of a smile passes over his drooling mouth.

'Ripley,' he sighs.

She has never heard her own name, and repeats it – like a spasm, she sees that scene in *Aliens* where the shreds of Bishop save Newt from being swept away.

'Newt,' she says, haltingly. 'Newt is gone.'

'They're all gone,' stammers Bishop; his speech function has deteriorated. 'But you're still here. What have you done?'

'Done?'

'The man who looks like me.'

'Off,' she answers.

And a look of contentment comes over Bishop's face. 'Good,' he says. 'I never could. I was programmed to see him as my father.'

'Me?' she asks.

'Go to the screens,' says Bishop, and his eyeballs roll leftwards to indicate a bank of video screens. She goes over to them, sees her own face reflected in the blank screen, reaches out to touch it, and lo, the screen comes to life with pictures.

It is a scene of some huge pit, filled and congested with alien monsters. Ripley is amazed at what she sees, but she feels no horror. Some atavistic impulse of recognition is at work. She whimpers, like an infant cut off from parents, and at that noise the monsters in the picture stir and slouch towards the camera, seeing her. They begin to roar their greetings, and her eyes widen in wonder.

18

Ripley throws off the alien on her face. Christie lobs grenades at the circle of eggs. As they burn, the others scramble up a ladder above the pool. There is a door at the top of the ladder, and Wren and Call lead the way in trying to open it. But when Call hands Wren her gun, so that she can work the door, he shoots her in the chest and makes his own escape. Call's body pitches back into the water, apparently dead.

Wren has closed the door behind him, of course. And now an especially ill-tempered alien prepares to get at the survivors who are trapped on the staircase. This alien plunges back into the water and then makes a determined running jump that lands it on the staircase, where it snaps at Christie and Vriess. In fact, as they are strapped together, Vriess is now hanging on to the rungs of the ladder while Christie seems like his appendage. The alien has hold of Christie's foot. Johner leans backwards and shoots at another alien. Then Christie's alien turns up the heat by spitting in his face – these aliens have learned to spit acid. Christie's face is badly wounded, and finally, to save Vriess, he unbuckles the harness that holds them together and then takes out his knife to cut through the last belt. He and the alien plunge down into the water, but Vriess is saved.

But still the door remains closed, until the survivors hear action behind it. It slides up, revealing the figure of Call, alive again, come to save them. Amid banal expressions of astonishment, Ripley finds the chest wound that had accounted for Call, puts in her hand and feels the white foam and wiring of a robot. Despite their peril, the company stand around for a few moments and marvel at how lifelike Call is, deciding which make and model she must be. Johner is aghast at thinking he might have fucked her!

A sceptic is bound to add that, if Winona Ryder was added to this film to help bring in the young crowd, still the actress was lumbered with a thankless part. Call has no crucial place in the action; she has no distinct affect; and, if she did, it would only detract from the proper attention that needs to be paid to Ripley. Added to which, Ms Ryder can leave us all in some doubt as to whether she is playing a human or a robot.

19

It may seem that events on the *Narcissus* are on a divergent course from those on the *Auriga*. Not so. I am happy to have the two pictures as close together, and as much in harmony, as railway tracks.

The *Narcissus* has been invented only to help make up for some shortcomings in the *Auriga*, to give more reality to Ripley's new status as a clone, and to pursue the deeper logic and coherence of the series. You may not like or appreciate the story of the *Narcissus* – but nor did the general public much enjoy the tale of the *Auriga* and the *Betty*.

Whatever, as events aspire to a climax, I am more than willing to have my Ripley fall in line with the one in *Alien Resurrection*. In other words, she leaves Bishop's tumultuous office, in search of her kin (or kindred spirits). Since I have never forgotten the strange charm of those shots in *Alien³* where Ripley had the remains of android Bishop slung over her shoulder, I would suggest that she takes him/it with her. The relationship between Ripley and the two Bishops is too rich to abandon. More than that, in a gesture of goodwill and reconciliation, I am prepared to have Ripley exchange the long white sheet – not the most practical garb for what is to come – for her brown leather outfit (Peterman's notion of what a biker groupie on Highway 1 should wear). How do we do that? We simply have a writer who can manage a change of clothes without undue fuss. What are writers for?

And then we have Ripley make her way from the penthouse levels down to the bowels of the ship – let the *Narcissus* now be renamed the *Auriga* – where the aliens are ready to riot. In the elevator on the way down, Bishop can tell Ripley that there is an escape craft ready to go (the *Betty*, why not?) because the *Auriga* is now set to self-destruct (because of the rioting aliens).

So Ripley slips back into our story. There are a few problems. *Alien Resurrection* still has Wren, Distephano, Johner, Vriess, Purvis and Call left. The working definition of dead wood, you may say, so let us allow *Resurrection* to have one more sequence of its own to clear the way. By the close of these films Ripley has no great need of ordinary company.

20

Let us, by all means, endorse the rather pretty way in which Wren is dispatched by the very monster that leaps out of Purvis's chest – this is a nice touch of self-sacrifice, and a properly gruesome way for Wren to go. Two down. Is it really beyond our wits to have Distephano picked off along the way? Johner could split an infinitive and fall upon its broken ends. Vriess? Well, Vriess could volunteer to pilot the *Auriga* away so that its inevitable explosion occurs somewhere off in harmless space. (As it is, the *Auriga* hits Earth and blows, causing a bang bigger than the one in the Yucatan that may have killed off our first dinosaurs.) And surely the crippled Vriess would need a robot to help him – in which case we're rid of Call, too. If there's one thing we've learned in a hundred years of cinema it is that we can kill anyone.

So Ripley comes alone (or with Bishop as the parrot on her shoulder) to the great lair of the alien monsters. And, here, we are as one with *Resurrection*, where a claw reaches up, pulls down the floor grating, and Ripley drops into the seething coils of monsters, monsters everywhere. She even slips beneath the surface, like someone drowning.

And *Resurrection* rises to something like mystery and marvel as it shows us Ripley reunited with the Queen that was drawn from her body. They caress. Then we realise that we are in a grotto – the birthing room, let's call it. There are cocoons hung up on the wall of the room that contain the other crew members of the *Auriga*. And one of these is Gediman, whose plaintive voice and unbroken scientific curiosity delight in telling Ripley that the exchange has been more than they ever anticipated. Just as Ripley has acquired acid for blood, a raging libido, and other alien attitudes, so the Queen has developed a human reproductive system.

The camera draws back and we see that the Queen is pregnant – that her belly harbours a heaving sac from which some creature is bursting to be delivered. The decision to take the story there seems to me true and penetrating – this is what the fourth film should do. And the scene in which Ripley greets the mother is as touching as it is startling.

21

But then the fourth film goes astray. The birthing occurs, and we see a creature that is a version of King Kong (as opposed to the Queen), even if it is scaled and slimy. This is not a reptile. It stands like an ape. It has a head and arms. It has eyes. As a matter of fact, this alien is in the cast list, and is played by Tom Woodruff, Jr, one of the men responsible for the overall design of the 'alien effects'. It may be Mr Woodruff's eyes – sad and smart, I judge – that we see behind the rather ill-fitting mask of the monster's face. This is the first alien in the series, I suggest, that does not quite work – which risks bathos or even inadvertent comedy.

Still, the child does its best. It turns on its own mother and kills her. Instead, it seeks to deliver its affection, its love, to Ripley. It comes towards her. It sniffs her, and then it lets out its yard or so of tongue to lick her face. Sigourney Weaver is not quite instinctive enough to let this seem like the highest moment of Ripley's life.

Indeed, as the alien turns on Gediman and bites off his head, Ripley gets away. She runs towards the *Betty* and manages a terrific long jump across its ramp just as the craft is about to pull away. Of course, Call, Johner and Vriess are on board, but they gladly surrender the controls to Ripley.

Except that her grandchild has come, too.

And so there is a last conflict on board the *Betty* in which Ripley uses her own blood to burn a hole in the porthole window so that, bit by bit, the shreds and pieces, the entirety of the monster, are sucked out into space. While Call and Ripley just hang on.

Of course, a punctured ship would lose everything under those circumstances, but I will not cavil. The gradual extrusion of the screaming monster is very well done. And Ripley's grief matches it. The scene works – even if Ripley has forsaken her mixed nature now and goes back to being a good officer. Indeed, Call says to her, 'We saved the Earth.' And we see the bright blue planet towards which the *Betty* is headed. We are aimed at Texas, it seems.

There are shots of clouds, lit up by a sunrise. These are the first shots taken in unequivocal natural light in the whole quartet.

'What happens now?' asks Call.

'I don't know,' says Ripley. 'I'm a stranger here myself.' Which again is the line of someone who's seen too many movies, but who may be thinking of *Alien 5* – or maybe it should be *Aliens 5, Earth 0*?

22

Something is lost, I think, when the Queen gives birth to the monster. May I suggest this alternative? As the sac heaves and as the life within it struggles to emerge, an arm breaks through. It may be a scaled arm, but a human arm, and what emerges with it is a sleek human being – it would have been an amazing coup to have Winona Ryder in *this* part – crop-haired, wide-eyed, naked and slimy, herself to all intents and purposes but with just a few extra-human touches. Scales like epaulets perhaps? A vampire's teeth? One whiplash tail? And a voice such as no human has ever uttered, filled with the elemental need for existence. Then Ripley moves towards this figure, cradles it, and begins to lick it clean of the birth mucous. The new child staggers to its feet, like a colt, so wild, so innocent, so dangerous, so wondrous.

I would have the film end with the *Betty* coming down to Earth – it might be in the dunes of Death Valley, or in the midst of Yosemite. No other people exist. But in the meadow or the desert, Ripley teaches her pristine grandchild to stand erect. Their roars dispel the silence.

Four Times Upon a Time . . .

Alien Resurrection caused no excitement. Opening at Thanksgiving, it was hard to find by Christmas. There was a moderate first week, then its business fell off fast. By the end of the year it had done only a little over $40 million, with nothing else in sight. The reviews called it cold, ugly, harsh and uninvolving, and they made little or no effort to relate it to the earlier films. None of the admirers of the series could honestly claim that the baton (or the meaning) had been passed on. There was a sense of bitter dismay in *Alien* fans. Yet in the month that followed December 19th, Fox's *Titanic* earned nearly $250 million. At the moment of *Resurrection*'s opening there had been boisterous talk of a fifth film; a month later, no one wanted to get into that topic. In the new year, as studios made videocassettes to send out to the members of the Academy, Fox took the decision to make no tapes for *Alien Resurrection*. And it was the first picture in the series that earned no nomination for visual effects.

Yet it picked up overseas: foreign earnings were close to $100 million – enough for the studio to scrape by. But 5 now was a pipe-dream such as only one man could command – James Cameron.

For Sigourney Weaver, if for no one else, Academy indifference was a hard verdict. The new Ripley was a very challenging role, calling for human and inhuman characteristics. Her effort was not always helped by the script or the direction, yet in many scenes Weaver's performance was exceptional and moving. She did suggest another kind of being, uncertain of her own nature or allegiances. She had brought the odyssey of Ellen Ripley to an unnerving point just as she had carried her primal conflict with the alien as far as a strange kind of marriage. The human being had been altered, but the alien was different, too. And there might have been a story and a movie that had a fuller sense of that. As it was, for the third time, we had to watch an alien tossed out into the endlessly available space, rather than be absorbed.

Over the years, many people engaged on the *Alien* films had spoken about the need to explain the aliens – where they came from, how they were made, why they were so 'hostile', what they wanted. That was always an understandable mistake. As both figures on a screen and entities in a story, they had a magnificence, an arbitrariness, that would have been spoiled by explanation. Far more important than any causative, narrative answer to how they had acid for blood was their living up to the legendary status of being endlessly renewable, nasty, dangerous and beyond reason. To be alien is to be unknowable. And yet in any kingdom, or story, of amazing futuristic intelligence, the unknowable is as valuable intellectually as anti-intelligence, anti-matter or a great black hole that wants to suck away all things and edifices.

   That is why I have tried to pose, from early on in the series, a curious kind of attraction – as much electronic as erotic – between Ripley and the alien. The attraction of pure opposites that has time and space to go beyond instinctive combat. Remember how, in *Alien*, Sigourney Weaver felt that moment when the beast saw her not quite as a cutie in her underwear but as a way 'of following its natural instincts to reproduce through whatever living things are around it'. It's a little like the force of evil (if you were disposed to consider such a thing) or the denial of reason and hope, seeing that it might as well take on a human form.

   It's no wonder, over the years, that several people entertained the idea of an alien that could become whatever thing it attacked – all living creatures, and even such large and unmanageable things as a field of corn or a sheet of glass. Imagine the potential of such things possessed by evil and you are not far from certain great moments in Hitchcock, say – the empty prairie where Cary Grant waits in *North by Northwest*, or the heights of San Francisco in *Vertigo*, a city increasingly drained of real life to be replaced by spell.

If only, one feels like saying, one person could have conceived the whole thing, all four parts, and executed it faithfully. But movies are not like that, much less series of movies or ones that loom as large financially as the *Alien* pictures. Anyone imagining what the film means, or might mean, has to be reconciled to the relentless confusion, interference, disorder, waywardness – whatever – of films made as they are made. But there is a special charm to the meaning of these films that it was not just never delivered, but never grasped by any one person. Rather, the meaning is a possibility that hovers over the immaculate imagery. If you doubt that power of possibility, play the game in a group: let every person tell the story of *Alien 5* – I guarantee there will not be a dull story in the bunch. For there is a pregnancy there now that understands the fruitfulness where stories actually told blend in with all the other stories there might have been.

You can say that 2, 3 or 4 went off in a wrong direction – only the original escapes that charge. You can say that 3 and 4 should have accelerated the combat of 2 – but that might have become absurd in ten minutes. Some say 3 was the seed of entropy because it killed Ripley – yet I hope I have shown how far Ripley's death lets us enter into fresh prospects. After all, cinema has always played odd games with life and death; it is a medium filled with ghostliness, and we ought to be grown up enough by now to deal with the haunting glow that comes off Ripley's features as well as the prospects in cloning. There may be nothing so metaphysically intriguing in this quartet as its repeated request 'Kill me, kill me' and Ripley's amused understanding that, having died once, she is no longer threatened by the alien in its old way. There is a limited escape in death.

It may be that the word 'resurrection' was used in the title of film 4 as a gimmick – without thought, let alone reverence – but, yet again, a legend can surpass its makers. The idea of rebirth, or of transcending mere death, is out there, even if it involves a new reach in science that, so far, we are inclined to disdain. As if the human race had ever shown much capacity for disregarding the dangerous things it invented or discovered. And the thought of cloning in a movie only reminds us that photography and cinematography were cloning devices long before the word or the process, let alone its danger, were active in science. The photograph defies death, after all, and it introduces us into the realm of the lifelike ditto device that lasts after death. That is why, by now, the four *Alien* movies, made over a period of eighteen years, and earning over $300 million, are coexistent, four times upon a time. How interesting it would be to see the four films projected simultaneously and on the four walls of one room.

In addition, this short book has tried to detail the actual vagaries of film-making – the compromises in authorship, collaboration, budget, etc. that seem to impede the sweet flow of the myth. But the myth is like water in a river: it goes wherever it can and must, and it knows that the twists and turns are as pretty – and every bit as river-like – as the long, straight, serene stretches. We cannot expect film-making to be anything other than what it is – which doesn't mean that we should refrain from remarking on its greed, its idiocy, its cowardice, or its 'mistakes'. There is film commentary in this book that actively reworks one movie and tries to coax it out of its known course. That's stupid but legitimate, I think, and only a late (or belated) addition to the process of change that went on while the picture was being made. A legend is all its variations – those written but unused, those filmed but discarded, those imagined but never realised.

And sometimes movie has a way of delivering profound myths without benefit of good or great films. The history of film has given us so many unforgettable dreams that do not have to be masterpieces, or works of art, or even box-office hits. To name a few: *King Kong, Frankenstein, Vertigo, Blue Velvet, The Night of the Hunter* – films in which something very naive is fused with something deeply mysterious. And these may be the best that film has ever done: to leave us uncertain about the boundaries of low art and high art. The *Alien* films are shockers in the old-fashioned sense of showmanship, carnival and freak shows. But they are also religious meditations on the body and the soul, and on how one can break and be invaded without the other being given up.

What does the series mean – for science fiction, horror or the movies? Does it need to mean anything? Maybe it is enough to ask questions. In which case, I would point to the end of *Alien Resurrection* where a clone and an android save the Earth. In life, we face the company of clones and artificial intelligences; in movie, we are seeing an end to photography and the onset of electronic or special effects. We have to judge whether that change is a sign to the future – or a warning? Take that as the legacy of Ripley's believe it or not.

Filmography

ALIEN, 1979

directed by Ridley Scott; produced by Gordon Carroll, David Giler and Walter Hill; executive producer, Ronald Shusett; associate producer, Ivor Powell; production executive, Mark Haggard; production manager, Garth Thomas; assistant directors, Paul Ibbetson, Raymond Becket, Steve Harding.

screenplay by Dan O'Bannon; story by Dan O'Bannon and Ronald Shusett.

photography by Derek Vanlint and Denys Ayling (miniatures); camera operator, David Litchfield; editors, Terry Rawlings, Peter Weatherly; production designer, Michael Seymour; art direction, Les Dilley, Roger Christian; visual design consultant, Dan O'Bannon; set decorator, Ian Whittaker; Alien design, H. R. Giger; small forms, H. R. Giger, Roger Dicken; Alien head effects, Carlo Rambaldi; music, Jerry Goldsmith, with extracts from 2nd Symphony by Howard Hanson.

Dallas	Tom Skerritt
Ripley	Sigourney Weaver
Lambert	Veronica Cartwright
Brett	Harry Dean Stanton
Kane	John Hurt
Ash	Ian Holm
Parker	Yaphet Kotto
Voice of 'Mother'	Helen Horton
Alien	Bolaji Badejo

117 mins; Eastman Colour, prints by De Luxe; Panavision; production company, 20th Century-Fox, a Brandywine–Ronald Shusett Production; distributed by 20th Century-Fox.

ALIENS, 1986

aadirected by James Cameron; produced by Gale Anne Hurd; executive producers, Gordon Carroll, David Giler and Walter Hill; production supervisor, Hugh Harlow; assistant directors, Derek Cracknell, Melvin Lind.

screenplay by James Cameron; story by James Cameron and David Giler and Walter Hill.

photography by Adrian Biddle; editor, Ray Lovejoy; production designer, Peter Lamont; Alien effects, Stan Winston; certain special effects, The L.A. Effects Group Inc.; visual effects supervisors, Robert Skotak, Dennis Skotak; visual effects supervisor (post-production), Brian Johnson; special effects supervisor, John Richardson; 2nd unit director, Stan Winston; costumes, Emma Porteous; music, James Horner.

Ripley	Sigourney Weaver
Newt	Carrie Henn
Cpl Hicks	Michael Biehn
Burke	Paul Reiser
Bishop	Lance Henriksen
Pvt Hudson	Bill Paxton
Lt Gorman	William Hope
Pvt Vasquez	Jenette Goldstein
Sgt Apone	Al Matthews
Pvt Drake	Mark Rolston
Pvt Frost	Rocco Ross
Cpl Ferro	Colette Hiller
Pvt Spunkmayer	Daniel Kash
Cpl Dietrich	Cynthia Scott
Pvt Crowe	Tip Tipping
Pvt Wierzowski	Trevor Steedman
Van Leuwen	Paul Maxwell
ECA Rep	Valerie Colgan
Insurance man	Alan Polonsky
Nurse	Alibe Parsons
Cocooned woman	Barbara Coles
Alien warrior	Carl Toop
Power loader operator	John Lees

136 mins;* Eastman Colour; prints by De Luxe; production company, 20th Century-Fox, a Brandywine Production; distributed by 20th Century-Fox.

*A longer cut, of 153 minutes, is available on laser-disc.

ALIEN³, 1992

directed by David Fincher; produced by Gordon Carroll, David Giler and Walter Hill; co-producer, Sigourney Weaver; executive producer, Ezra Swerdlow; production supervisor, Patricia Carr; assistant director, Chris Carreras.

screenplay by David Giler and Walter Hill and Larry Ferguson; story by Vincent Ward.

photography by Alex Thomson; editor, Terry Rawlings; production design, Norman Reynolds; costumes, Bob Ringwood, David Perry; visual effects, Richard Edlund; *Alien³* creature design by H. R. Giger; alien effects, Alec Gillis, Tom Woodruff, Jr; special effects supervisor, George Gibbs; music, Elliot Goldenthal.

Ripley	Sigourney Weaver
Dillon	Charles S. Dutton
Clemens	Charles Dance
Bishop	Lance Henriksen
Golic	Paul McGann
Andrews	Brian Glover
Aaron	Ralph Brown
Morse	Danny Webb
Rains	Christopher John Fields
Junior	Holt McCallany
Murphy	Chris Fairbank
Frank	Carl Chase
Boggs	Leon Herbert
Jude	Vincenzo Nicoli
David	Pete Postlethwaite
Troy	Paul Brennen
William	Clive Mantle
Gregor	Peter Guinness
Arthur	Dhobi Oparei
Kevin	Philip Davis
Eric	Niall Buggy
Company man	Hi Ching
Newt	Danielle Edmond

115 mins; Eastman Colour; prints by Rank; production company, 20th Century-Fox, a Brandywine Production; distributed by 20th Century-Fox.

ALIEN RESURRECTION,
1997

directed by Jean-Pierre Jeunet; produced by Bill Badalato, Gordon Carroll, David Giler and Walter Hill; executive producer, Sigourney Weaver; production supervisor, Bob Johnston; co-production supervisor, Billy Badalato; production manager, Bill Badalato; assistant directors, Michel Cheyko, Mark Oppenheimer, Nancy King.

screenplay by Joss Whedon.

photography by Darius Khondji; camera operator, Conrad Hall; editor, Herve Schneid; production designer, Nigel Phelps; art direction, Andrew Nekoromny; visual effects supervisor, Pitof and Eric Henry; Alien effects, Alec Gillis, Tom Woodruff, Jr; music John Frizzell.

Ripley	Sigourney Weaver
Call	Winona Ryder
Vriess	Dominique Pinon
Johner	Ron Perlman
Christie	Gary Dourdan
Elgyn	Michael Wincott
Hillard	Kim Flowers
General Perez	Dan Hedaya
Dr Wren	J. E. Freeman
Gediman	Brad Dourif
Distephano	Raymond Cruz
Purvis	Leland Orser
Young Ripley	Nicole Fellows
Lead Alien	Tom Woodruff, Jr

108 mins; Colour by De Luxe; Panavision; production company, 20th Century-Fox, a Brandywine Production; distributed by 20th Century-Fox.

Bibliography

Abramowitz, Rachel, 'Leave it to Weaver' (interview), *Premiere* (Women in Hollywood issue), 1998

Andrews, Nigel and Kennedy, Harlan, 'Space Gothic', *American Film*, March 1979.

Carducci, Mark Patrick, Lovell, Glenn, Clarke, Frederick S., Fox, Jordan R., Jones, Alan and Levy, Frederic Albert, 'Making Alien: Behind the Scenes', *Cinefantastique*, vol. 9, no. 1

Eaton, Michael, 'Born Again', *Sight and Sound*, December 1997

Fox, Jordan R., 'Carpenter: Riding High on Horror', *Cinefantastique*, Summer 1980

Giger, H. R., *www HR Giger com*, Taschen, 1997

Hobby, Patrick and Teitelbaum, Sheldon, 'Alien 3 – It Came from Development Hell', *Cinefantastique*, June 1992

Kutzera, Dale, 'Alien 4: Resurrection', *Cinefantastique*, December 1997

Mooney, Joshua, 'Lasting Impact: Interview with James Cameron', *Movieline*, July 1994

Murdock, Andrew and Aberly, Rachel, *The Making of Alien Resurrection*, Harper Prism, 1997

Murphy, Kathleen, 'The Last Temptation of Sigourney Weaver', *Film Comment*, July–August 1992

Pally, Marcia, 'Sigourney Takes Control', *Film Comment*, December 1986

Peary, Danny, 'Playing Ripley in *Alien*: Interview with Sigourney Weaver', *Omni's Screen Flights/Screen Fantasies*, Doubleday, 1984

Peary, Danny, 'Directing *Alien* and *Blade Runner*: Interview with Ridley Scott', ibid.

Rebello, Stephen, 'Tales of an Alien Director', *Movieline*, November 1997

Rebello, Stephen, 'The Heat Is On: Interview with Sigourney Weaver', *Movieline*, June 1992

Rebello, Stephen, 'Ripley's Game: Interview with Sigourney Weaver', *Movieline*, September 1997

Silver, Alain J. and Ward, Elizabeth, 'Scriptwriter and Director: Interview with Walter Hill', *Movie*, no. 26

Smith, Gavin, 'Don't Let That Go – That's Valuable', Interview with Lance Henriksen, *Film Comment*, September–October 1993.

Taubin, Amy, 'Invading Bodies', *Sight and Sound*, July 1992

David Thomson, born and educated in London, now lives in San Francisco. He writes regularly for both the U.S. edition of *Esquire* and the *Indepdendent on Sunday* in London. He is also known for his biographies – *Showman: The Life of David O. Selznick* and *Rosebud: The Story of Orson Welles* – for three remarkable 'fictions' that are derived from the screen – *Suspects, Silver Light* and *Warren Beatty and Desert Eyes* – and for *A Biographical Dictionary of Film*, which is now in its third edition. His most recent book is *Beneath Mulholland*, a collection of essays, and he is also the author of *4–2* (from Bloomsbury), a memoir on growing up as a soccer fan, based on the 1966 World Cup final.

Index

in *Aliens*, 59, 63–94, 96
in *Alien³*, 100–01, 105–31
in *Alien Resurrection*, 134–37,
 143–69, 170–71
almost not in *Alien³*, 98
attitude to voyeuristic
 scenes, 57–58
attitude to weapons, 100,
 132–33, 152
basketball training, 150
career of, 34–35
casting of, 2, 10–12, 15
as clone Number 7, 159
conveying of emotion, 111
as executive producer, 135,
 143, 152
fan letters, 54
legal action against Fox, 98
Oscar nomination, 96
script ideas for *Alien³*, 100
self denial in baldness,
 101, 117
and the shooting of *Alien*, 14
thoughts on the cloned
 Ripley, 151–52, 154
see also Ripley

Webb, Danny, 123
Weyland-Yutani (the
 Company), 131
 see also Company, the
Whedon, Joss, 134–35
White Squall, 10
Who'll Stop the Rain, 77
Wierzowski, Marine, 72
Wigan, Gareth, 11
Wincott, Michael, 148
Winston, Stan, 59, 96, 100
Wise Blood, 11
Women, in Scott's films,
 10–11, 57
Woodruff, Tom Jr., 101,
 136, 168
Working Girl, 101
World of Suzie Wong, The, 6
Wren, Dr., 142, 146, 148, 154,
 155, 158, 164, 167

*Year of Living Dangerously,
 The*, 59

Z Cars, 8